English Exposed

English Exposed

Common Mistakes Made by Chinese Speakers

Steve Hart

HKU PRESS
香港大學出版社

CONTENTS

Preface

> Failure is instructive. The person who really thinks, learns quite as much from his failures as from his successes.
>
> —John Dewey

John Dewey realized that just as much can be learnt from doing things badly as from doing things well—and this certainly applies to writing in English. English is not an easy language to master, especially if it is being learnt as a second or third language. But improving written English skills can be achieved if instruction is given on where to look for problems and then feedback provided on how to solve them.

As an academic proofreader, I have read and edited over 600 papers written by Chinese undergraduates, postgraduates, and researchers. Three years ago I decided to analyse the most common errors[1] found in these papers so Chinese writers of English could improve their skills. Because each of the examples I analysed was a real-world example, and had actually been written by a Chinese student/researcher writing in English,[2] I thought it would be the perfect material for a learning resource and an opportunity to put Dewey's idea that people really can learn a lot from their mistakes—and from the mistakes of others—into practice. English Exposed is the outcome of this process.

The mistakes made by writers[3] are examined by grammar area, term selection, and by elements found in an essay such as figures, punctuation, and referencing. Naturally there is some overlap, but readers can see what topics and what errors feature at the start of each chapter, and they can find specific topics and terms via the indexes and the cross-referencing found throughout.

To ensure that the example errors are as instructive as possible, solutions are provided directly beneath them and explanations are given. Background

---

1. Errors that occurred in at least 5% of the papers were considered 'common'. This meant the error had to have been made by at least thirty writers.
2. Where necessary, the wording of the example has been altered to preserve anonymity while retaining the nature of the error.
3. The term 'writer' used throughout the book refers to a writer whose first language is not English.

information on each grammar area is provided and exercises can be found at the end of each chapter to support the learning process and embed this knowledge.

There are three main parts to the resource.

Classes. This category looks at errors made in each general grammar class. The parts of speech are explored and the most common errors revealed and addressed.

Choices. This section focuses on confusion about word choice. It features related and unrelated terms and how to rid writing of unnecessary and inappropriate phrases.

Components. This part addresses different elements that comprise an essay or a paper, such as using numbers, tables, punctuation, and references. Useful areas such as dates, time phrases, and referring to countries are also explored.

All content has been designed specifically for those writers looking to fine-tune their language skills and create error-free academic English. It must be frustrating for good research skills and strong subject knowledge to be undermined by weaker English writing ability. But if Dewey's advice is followed and mistakes are viewed as instructive, then English Exposed can empower Chinese writers of English to acquire an awareness of the mistakes they and their peers are making and, crucially, provide them with the knowledge to fix these errors and improve their written English level.

Acknowledgements

I wish to thank Susie Han for her enthusiasm, diligence, and swift correspondence on this project.

Steve Hart
2016

About the Author

Steve Hart has been editing and proofreading for international academics and graduate students since 2005. He has co-authored undergraduate English text-books and written two practical grammar guides for university students. He is currently an academic English coordinator and dissertation supervisor at a higher education institution in Cambridge, England.

Part A

Classes . . . to recognize

1
COUNTABLE AND UNCOUNTABLE NOUNS

Focus on . . . Countable nouns

Uncountable nouns

Plural noun forms

This chapter analyses the differences between countable and uncountable nouns and explains why some nouns can be both countable and uncountable. It also explores problematic plural noun endings along with errors that are typically made in this area.

Background / 1.1 'evidence' and dividing uncountable nouns /
1.2 number and amount / 1.3 plural noun endings /
1.4 countable and uncountable nouns / 1.5 phrases and plural nouns /
1.6 Exercises

Usage errors exposed in 1:

abilities (1.4)
amount (1.2)
attention (1.1)
belief (1.3)
by means of (1.5)
caution (1.1)
clothes (1.3)
communication (1.4)
competition (1.4)
contents (1.4)

crisis (1.3)
evidence (1.1)
for example (1.5)
for instance (1.5)
in detail (1.5)
in practice (1.5)
in theory (1.5)
many (1.1)
number (1.2)
phenomena (1.3)

research (1.1)
strength (1.4)
strengthen (1.4)
weakness (1.4)

BACKGROUND: If a noun can be counted, it will have a clear boundary (physically or conceptually) and will be seen as a separate entity.

*There were several **managers** present at the meeting.*

A manager can be counted because it is a person and is clearly a separate thing. But countable nouns do not have to exist physically in the real world.

*A few more **models** were developed to try to resolve this issue.*

Although some ideas and inanimate things can be countable and therefore plural, most concepts and notions will be uncountable. An uncountable noun means no boundary or limit can be formed for it; that is why these nouns are commonly qualities, feelings, and social processes.

*There was **confusion** because the government had previously acknowledged that the problem was not a financial one.*

REVEALED: 1.1 *– How to use 'evidence' properly and how to divide an uncountable noun*

'Evidence' is an uncountable noun but what does uncountable actually mean?

First, an uncountable noun cannot have a plural form.

*We collected **evidences** about the behaviour and then grouped **them** according to **their** severity.* ✘

*We collected **evidence** about the behaviour and then grouped **it** according to **its** severity.* ✔

> **!** When correcting this error, all the verbs and pronouns have to be in singular form to reflect the uncountable nature of the noun.
>
> *The evidence **is** useful, and **it** can be . . .*

Second, the uncountable noun cannot take an indefinite article ('a' / 'an').

*There was **an evidence** of this after the model was initially tested.* ✘

Other uncountable nouns that are mistakenly used as countable nouns include:

> advice   attention   caution   confidence   confusion   health   help
> information   research   safety   support   training   transport   trust

> **!** Remember that none of the nouns above can be used in plural form.
>
> advices   attentions   cautions . . .
>
> *The team has carried out a number of researches.* ✗
> *The team has carried out a number of **studies**.* ✔
>
> *A lot of attentions have been paid to this subject in recent years.* ✗
> *A lot of **attention has** been paid to this subject in recent years.* ✔
>
> *They should therefore proceed with cautions.* ✗
> *They should therefore proceed with **caution**.* ✔

Sometimes it is necessary to divide the uncountable noun into individual parts or different types. Certain quantity phrases can be used to do this.

> *There was **some** evidence of this after the model was initially tested.*
> *There are different **types** of evidence that can be used in this situation.*

> *Different evidences were required.* ✗
> *Different **types of evidence** were required.* ✔

Note that the verb must agree with the phrase expressing quantity. Here, a plural verb is required.

> *Three pieces of advice I received **were** . . .*
> *Two different kinds of research **have** . . .*

▷ RELATED ERRORS:

A common error is to use an uncountable noun as a plural with the term 'many'.

> *Many evidences have been found to link obesity with the eating habits of parents.*

'Many' is used with countable nouns. Uncountable nouns will usually require 'much'. The verb will need to be singular as well.

> **Much evidence has** *been found to link obesity* . . .

(See Chapter 3 for more quantity phrases.)

REVEALED: 1.2 – *When to use 'number' and when to use 'amount'*

The countability of the noun determines whether 'number' or 'amount' should be used. In this first example 'studies' is plural, so 'number' is the correct choice.

> *In contrast,* **an amount of** *studies have investigated the efficiency of smaller banks.* ✗
>
> *In contrast,* **a number of** *studies have investigated the efficiency of smaller banks.* ✔   (See 3.2.)

'Amount' is used with uncountable nouns. In the next example 'development' is employed in an uncountable way (it can also be countable), and so the writer correctly uses 'amount'.

> *This should also result in a greater* **amount** *of development taking place.*

See 16.7 for an explanation of when to use 'fewer' and 'less' and 3 for more quantity phrases.

REVEALED: 1.3 – *How to form plural noun endings*

Many plural nouns are formed by adding 's' or 'es' to the singular noun.

> *subject, subjects   design, designs   approach, approaches*

But there are also nouns that have irregular endings, and writers need to recognize these.

The countable noun 'phenomenon' has a plural form that is written 'phenomena'. Writers either use the plural form as a singular noun, as in the following example:

> *This* **phenomena** *is prevalent in the villages and remote areas.* ✗
>
> *This* **phenomenon** *is prevalent in the villages and remote areas.* ✔

Or they add an 's' to form the incorrect plural, *phenomenons*.

It is important to remember that a plural noun requires a plural verb form.

> These phenomena **has** been investigated in other parts of the country as well. ✗
>
> These phenomena **have** been investigated in other parts of the country as well. ✔

*   *   *

Another noun that causes problems is 'belief'. This word has a regular ending. To form the plural, 's' is simply added; writers often commit the following error:

> Research was also carried out on their traditions and **believes**. ✗
>
> Research was also carried out on their traditions and **beliefs**. ✔

'Believes' is a verb form and not the plural form of the noun 'belief'. (See also 11.3.)

*   *   *

The plural form of 'crisis' is 'crises'. Often this change is not made to the plural.

> A number of economic **crisis** have hit the region in the past few decades. ✗
>
> A number of economic **crises** have hit the region in the past few decades. ✔

> Some nouns have only a plural form; for instance, 'clothes' has no singular form. Note the following errors.
>
> The company did not specifically ask them to wear their branded *cloths*. ✗
>
> The company did not specifically ask them to wear their branded **clothes**. ✔
>
> The *cloth* he wore was clearly authentic. ✗
>
> The **clothes** he wore were clearly authentic. ✔
>
> Normally, to refer to particular clothes a phrase such as 'piece of clothing' or 'item of clothing' is used.

REVEALED: 1.4 – *That some nouns can be both countable and uncountable*

A confusing point for many writers is that some nouns can be both countable and uncountable.

> *The company prefers the application to be written on **paper**.*
>
> *A number of **papers** had to be submitted before the end of term.*

The first example of the noun 'paper' is referring to the substance and is therefore uncountable. But in the second example, the writer is referring to specific essay papers which can naturally be counted (there are a number of them). Nouns that can be both countable and uncountable are often countable when a specific instance or kind is being referred to. They are uncountable when the general concept or sense is desired.

> *This clearly demonstrates that **absence** from class will lead to failure.* (general concept)
>
> *There were a number of **absences** from this group the week before as well.* (specific instances)

*   *   *

'Strength' is a noun that can be used in either a countable or an uncountable way.

Countable: a particular quality or ability (that is good or beneficial).

Uncountable: physical or mental power and energy; quality or state of being strong.

Writers often use the plural form instead of the required uncountable noun form.

> *These materials are frequently used in the industry because of their strengths.* ✗
>
> *These materials are frequently used in the industry because of their **strength**.* ✔

I➤ RELATED ERRORS:

The phrase 'strengths and weaknesses' attracts the following errors.

> *There are a number of strengths and weakness.* ✗
>
> *There are a number of strengths and **weaknesses**.* ✔

An evaluation of its ***strength*** *and* ***weakens*** *must then follow.* ✗

An evaluation of its ***strengths*** *and* ***weaknesses*** *must then follow.* ✔

When used together, the two nouns are usually plural unless used in the following way.

This is both a strength and a weakness.

Errors can also occur when the verb 'to strengthen' is required.

This ***strengths*** *the line sufficiently.* ✗

This ***strengthens*** *the line sufficiently.* ✔

They will also need to ***strength*** *the links between the two operators.* ✗

They will also need to ***strengthen*** *the links between the two operators.* ✔

Other nouns that can be either countable or uncountable are:

achievement behaviour control development experience
industry policy power society teaching theory

There is a tendency to overuse the plural with nouns that can be either countable or uncountable. Remember the uncountable form will be required when the phrase is referring to the general concept or attribute and not describing specific kinds or actual instances.

This will depend on their ***abilities*** *to detect errors.* ✗

This will depend on their ***ability*** *to detect errors.* ✔

Two nouns that seem to attract this error are 'competition' and 'communication'.

The plural form has been used in this first example when the meaning only relates to 'competition' in general.

In this framework, ***competitions*** *occurring within the industry are targeted.* ✗

In this framework, ***competition*** *occurring within the industry is targeted.* ✔

When used in the plural form or in the singular form with an indefinite article (see Chapter 2), this noun ('competition') takes on a slightly different meaning and relates to events or an actual event taking place—where individuals or groups compete for something.

There were various ***competitions*** *and workshops for the employees to take part in.*

This is also the case with 'communication'. Unless actual acts of communication are taking place or being described, or the field itself or a particular network is being referred to, the uncountable form is the likely choice.

> **Communications** *are vital between a patient and the carer.* ✗
>
> **Communication** *is vital between a patient and the carer.* ✔

Communication is not often used in a singular countable sense ('a communication'). As a plural it can be used to refer to infrastructure or the field as shown here.

> *The next section gives an overview of the signalling and* **communications** *they have developed on site.*
>
> *They studied computer networks and* **communications** *at university.*

▐➤ RELATED ERRORS:

The list of chapters and sections at the beginning of a paper is called the 'Contents'.

It outlines the 'content' of the paper.

> *The report will also require a 'Table of* **Content***'.* ✗
>
> *The report will also require a 'Table of* **Contents***'.* ✔

> *The tutor suggested that there was too much* **contents** *in the first section.* ✗
>
> *The tutor suggested that there was too much* **content** *in the first section.* ✔

REVEALED: 1.5 *– Phrases that should not contain a plural noun*

Singular and plural mistakes also occur in certain phrases. The terms in this section are 'fixed' and must be written in a specific way. (See 2.5 for an explanation of fixed phrases.)

The following must remain singular.

in detail

'Details' is the plural form of the noun 'detail'.

*The key **details** of this report can be found in the Appendix.*

'In detail' is a fixed phrase meaning 'item by item, or thoroughly'.

It should not be used as a plural.

*The findings will be discussed **in details** in the next section.* ✘
*The findings will be discussed **in detail** in the next section.* ✔

'More' can be inserted into the phrase, but again the term must remain singular.

*The following section will look at the process **in more details**.* ✘
*The following section will look at the process **in more detail**.* ✔

> Note that the phrase 'more details' is correct (without using 'in' at the start).
>
> ***More details** will be provided at a later stage.*
> *So,   In more detail* ✔   *More details* ✔

for example / for instance

*. . . **for examples**, BMI is a better predictor of hypertension.* ✘
*. . . **for example**, BMI is a better predictor of hypertension.* ✔

*. . . which includes classroom performance and assessment; **for instances**, the mid-term oral test . . .* ✘
*. . . which includes classroom performance and assessment; **for instance**, the mid-term oral test . . .* ✔

in theory / in reality / in practice

***In theories**, all the students could be asked to participate; **in practices**, the room is too small to accommodate them all.* ✘
***In theory**, all the students could be asked to participate; **in practice**, the room is too small to accommodate them all.* ✔

But this next phrase should be in the plural form.

by means of ('by using')

*This is navigated **by mean of** a small door at the back.* ✗

*This is navigated **by means of** a small door at the back.* ✔

> **!** This can often be shortened to just 'by'.
>
> *This was achieved **by means of** altering the middle section.* ✗
>
> *This was achieved **by** altering the middle section.* ✔

1.6 Exercises

A. Find the errors in these two paragraphs and correct them.

The issues related to healths and safety are discussed in the next section along with any informations from the respondents of the employee survey. The training schedule and transports advices for field trips are attached to the Appendices to provide more details, to avoid any confusion. The believes of the employees will be assessed, with a focus on whether they actually belief in the new policy.

The economic development of this region of China has aroused the interest of researchers of late. By means of SWOT analysis (which stands for strengthens, weakness, opportunities, and threats) I will assess the potential of the five SMEs from the area, with a focus on competition between the five regarding their capabilities. Any phenomena extracted from this analysis will form the basis for the second part of the study. Any experiences detailed by the business managers will also join those phenomenon as evidence to inform policy.

B. How many of these nouns can be used in a countable way (as a plural)?

advice   staff   training   support   behaviour   evidence   development

C. Pick one noun from above (B) that can be used in both a countable and an uncountable sense. Write two sentences containing the noun, one as a countable noun and the other as an uncountable noun.

Countable:

_____

Uncountable:

_____

2
ARTICLES

Focus on ... Articles

Countable nouns

Abbreviations

Fixed phrases

This chapter presents the different types of article occurring in English and introduces the concept of definiteness to understand which article should be used for which situation. The chapter reveals the most common mistakes and how they can be rectified. It also explores the relationship between articles and generic reference and explains what fixed phrases are.

Background / 2.1 singular countable nouns / 2.2 'a' or 'an'? /
2.3 definite article use / 2.4 indefinite article with plurals /
2.5 fixed phrases / 2.6 leaving out an article / 2.7 Exercises

Featured errors in 2:

a/an (2.2)	by name (2.5)
approach (2.1)	European (2.2)
as a result (2.5)	out of date (2.5)
at length (2.5)	researcher (2.1)
author (2.1)	study (2.1)
by email (2.5)	such (2.1)
by interview (2.5)	university (2.2)

BACKGROUND: An article is used before a noun to indicate the kind of reference being made to the noun.

the definite article = the

the indefinite article = a/an

the zero article = no article is used before the noun

Articles in English help the reader or listener to identify and follow the nouns in a sentence and to understand the relationship between them and the other parts of the sentence.

The best way to determine whether a definite article is needed is to ask the following questions:

Will the reader be aware of the exact thing I am referring to?

Do I want to, and am I able to, single out the noun as a unique instance?

If the answer is yes to both, then the noun is definite, and 'the' can be used before it.

__The changes__ were designed to make it easier to attract investment.

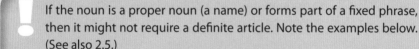

! If the noun is a proper noun (a name) or forms part of a fixed phrase, then it might not require a definite article. Note the examples below. (See also 2.5.)

The first case study is a company from __Hong Kong__.

They have analysed the policies of __PepsiCo__ from the US.

Most of the workers arrived __by bus__.

If the reader will not be able to identify (or more accurately, have 'awareness' of) the exact thing being described, or the writer wishes to be vague or to write generally, then the reference is said to be indefinite.

If the noun is used in an indefinite way, it will need either an indefinite article ('a'/'an') or a zero article (no article).

A singular countable noun takes an indefinite article when the reference is indefinite.

*A **theory** needs to be found that will help to explain this circumstance.*

A plural (countable) noun or an uncountable noun will take a zero article.

__Journals__ may also be a good source of information at this stage.

__Education__ is the main reason for the improvement we are currently seeing.

If the reference is definite (i.e., specific journals are being referred to or the education in a particular country is the subject), then a definite article is used.

__The journals__ in the office may also be a good source of information at this stage.

__The education__ in this country is below the level of its neighbours.

REVEALED: 2.1 – *That singular countable nouns always require an article*

Identifying whether a noun is countable or uncountable can be difficult, especially given that some nouns can be both (see 1.4). When a noun is used in a countable way and written in singular form, it will require either a definite article or an indefinite article—but it must have an article.

__Study__ by Morgan (2009) looked at the issue at a local level. ✗

__A study__ by Morgan (2009) looked at the issue at a local level. ✔

In the previous example, 'study' is countable so requires an article. (When it has an uncountable meaning, it will require a zero article, e.g., *Study is important for improving concentration in these pupils.*) As Morgan's study is being introduced, the writer has used an indefinite article.

> **!** In the plural form, a definite article can be used if the studies have been mentioned.
>
> *Six studies were randomly selected from the database for this stage. **The studies** were given a score out of five for their objectivity.*
>
> *But the plural noun would not require an article in a general context such as the one here (where the meaning is equivalent to 'some studies').*
>
> *__Studies__ have also focused on class size and the diversity of the pupils.*

When writers refer to themselves as 'researcher' or 'author' in their work, they often miss out the article. 'Researcher' and 'author' are singular countable nouns and require definite articles when they are directly referring to the writer of the paper or the research.

> **Researcher** *has demonstrated that practices in the country need to be in line with international ones.* ✘

> **The** *researcher has demonstrated that practices in the country need to be in line with international ones.* ✔

> *Because of this,* **author** *decided to rephrase question four.* ✘

> *Because of this,* **the** *author decided to rephrase question four.* ✔

One particular countable noun that always seems to be mistakenly written without an article is 'approach'.

> *We decided to use* **different approach** *this time.* ✘

A possible reason for missing out an article is that information modifying the noun (in the example above, the adjective different) has created a distraction.

> *We decided to use* **a different approach** *this time.* ✔

▷ RELATED ERRORS:

'Such' has a tendency to attract errors. When it is followed by a singular countable noun, an indefinite article should be used.

> **Such problem** *will not be solved in the short term.* ✘

> **Such a problem** *will not be solved in the short term.* ✔

An uncountable noun or a plural noun will not require an article.

> **Such development** *can only take place with extensive planning.*

> **Such problems** *will clearly affect their ability to attract investment.*

REVEALED: 2.2 – *When to use 'a' and 'an' with abbreviations and numbers*

Abbreviations have an interesting relationship with articles. The trick is to read each individual letter out loud, for instance SME (S 'es', M 'em', E 'e'). The sound of the first letter will determine whether 'a' or 'an' should be used.

> *Unfortunately, it is unlikely that **an** SME will be able to secure a loan under this scheme.*
>
> *This would not be the case for **a** PLC.*

> *I also spoke to **a MOD** employee.* ✘
>
> *I also spoke to **an MOD** employee.* ✔ ('M'= 'em')

For numbers, the spelling of the word will determine the article.

> ***An** 18-gauge needle* . . . (eighteen)

When a noun begins with 'eu' or 'u' and has a 'you' sound, 'a' is required.

> *The case study was that of **an** European country.* ✘
>
> *The case study was that of **a** European country.* ✔

> *It was not possible without **an** university degree.* ✘
>
> *It was not possible without **a** university degree.* ✔

REVEALED: 2.3 – *When not to use the definite article even though it seems the obvious choice*

Writers sometimes use 'the' without assessing whether the noun can be singled out as a unique instance.

> *This leaves an opportunity for **the** further study.* ✘
>
> *This leaves an opportunity for further study.* ✔

The error often occurs when writers are giving background information to something. They realize they are talking about a specific subject but fail to understand the indefinite and generic nature of the sentence. A definite article in these next examples would make the noun phrase unique, as if it was the only instance of its kind.

*China has **the** long history of developing this type of product for overseas markets.* ✘

*China has **a** long history of developing this type of product for overseas markets.* ✔

*As previously mentioned, this is **the** old culture and many traditions have been passed down through the generations.* ✘

*As previously mentioned, this is **an** old culture and many traditions have been passed down through the generations.* ✔

The second mention rule (use 'a' for the first mention and 'the' for the second mention of a noun) that is often taught in schools is the cause of many errors in sentences that are actually generic.

In this next example, the writer uses a zero article correctly in the first instance, but when mentioning the noun phrase again remembers the second mention rule and uses a definite article.

Brand loyalty (1) *is a broad area that has been extensively discussed in the marketing literature. This study will focus on **the** brand loyalty **(2)** and especially the concept of online brand advocacy.*

(1) The writer has correctly identified an uncountable and generic reading of the noun phrase (*brand loyalty*) so uses a zero article.

(2) The writer has noted that the term has already been used so opts for a definite article (because of the second mention rule) even though the noun is being used in exactly the same way as before and so will not require an article.

Failing to recognize generic meaning is a common error. In this next example the writer believes that, because she is writing about particular countries, a definite article is needed. But this has a generic reading, and therefore a zero article should be used.

*It is not just in Asia either, as they have also reported a prevalence of approximately 20%–25% in **the Western countries**.* ✘

*It is not just in Asia either, as they have also reported a prevalence of approximately 20%–25% **in Western countries**.* ✔

So, writers often fail to identify nouns being used in a general way. This is especially true if there are words modifying the noun. (See also 9.2.)

*A major aspect of **the customer service** is **the complaint resolution**.* ✘

*A major aspect of **customer service** is **complaint resolution**.* ✔

Perhaps surprisingly, a definite article is not usually required when defining a term or discussing a feature of it.

The promotional pricing is a form of sales promotion designed to increase product demand by offering a short-term price reduction. ✘

Promotional pricing is a form of sales promotion designed to increase product demand by offering a short-term price reduction. ✔

Note also that 'sales promotion' and 'product demand' above do not have articles before them.

See 17.1 for another example of where the definite article seems to be the obvious choice but is incorrect.

REVEALED: 2.4 – *The common mistake of using an indefinite article with a plural noun*

An unexpected error is using an indefinite article with a plural noun. It often occurs when there is information (modifying words) between the article and the noun.

*It has been important to utilize **a different contexts** for this.* ✘

*It has been important to utilize **different contexts** for this.* ✔

These modifiers should not distract the writer from making the correct article choice. It must always be informed by the noun, not necessarily the word coming directly after the article. These further examples will illustrate the point.

*These were all obtained from **a** semi-structured questionnaires.* ✘

These were all obtained from semi-structured questionnaires. ✔

*The problem with **an** additional and revised parameters is the inability to identify them during the later stages.* ✘

The problem with additional and revised parameters is the inability to identify them during the later stages. ✔

REVEALED: 2.5 – *What fixed phrases are and how to avoid the errors associated with them*

Fixed phrases are in general use and are familiar to native speakers. The particular words that feature in the phrase and their order are 'fixed'. Sometimes these phrases do not contain an article when one might be expected (e.g. by car). The meaning of these phrases may also be different from what one would assume. In other words, looking at the literal meaning of each word may not reveal the true meaning of the phrase (see also 1.5 which deals with phrases that should not contain a plural noun).

The preposition 'by' is often used before nouns in phrases that relate to transport, communication, and methods. No article is needed in these fixed phrases.

> *These were obtained **by the interview** after the questionnaires had been returned and analysed.* ✘

> *These were obtained **by interview** after the questionnaires had been returned and analysed.* ✔

> *I would also recommend doing this **by an email** instead or **by the post**.* ✘

> *I would also recommend doing this **by email** instead or **by post**.* ✔

in the case of/in case of

These two phrases look similar but have very different meanings. 'In case of' means 'if it should happen'. The phrase 'in the case of' means a particular case.

> *I suggested conducting the experiment indoors **in case of** rain.*

> *This could be as large as 40% **in the case of** developing countries.*

▶ RELATED ERRORS:

Here are some more examples where articles have been included in error.

> *Most of the literature they had used was **out of the date** even then.* ✘
> *Most of the literature they had used was **out of date** even then.* ✔

> *Morgan (1998) covered this **at a length** in his previous paper.* ✘
> *Morgan (1998) covered this **at length** in his previous paper.* ✔

*The headmaster also knew every one of the pupils **by the name**.* ✘

*The headmaster also knew every one of the pupils **by name**.* ✔

 Some fixed phrases do contain articles. Familiarization is key to selecting the correct one.

As the result, *financial institutions may be reluctant to lend to these firms.* ✘

As a result, *financial institutions may be reluctant to lend to these firms.* ✔

REVEALED: 2.6 – *Why an article can sometimes be left out and when this can be done*

Because scientists tend to describe general principles and processes in their work, the definite article is used sparingly in some technical papers.

Testing *of this product was carried out over three weeks.*

Things being tested are often stripped of their definite status and made generic despite the fact that specific events and actions are being described. This is especially true of plural nouns.

Target regions *were identified and* **drugs** *then added at regular intervals.* **Subjects** *were observed for one hour or until* **effects** *had worn off, whichever was sooner.*

In standard writing, the following definite articles would be expected.

The *target regions were identified and* **the** *drugs then added at regular intervals.* **The** *subjects were observed for one hour or until* **the** *effects had worn off, whichever was sooner.*

The problem with writing in the former style is the tendency to avoid using any articles at all, which could lead to writing that is imprecise and difficult to follow.

*Coefficient depends on **physical parameters** of soil. Image obtained was recorded and added to **survey**.* ✘

***The coefficient** depends on **the physical parameters of the soil. The image** obtained was recorded and added to **the survey**.* ✔

▶ RELATED ERRORS:

Often articles are omitted from titles and therefore from the contents page.

1.1	Nature of Learning Resources	3
1.2	Learning Resources in Context of Taiwan	5

Notice how in this next example the heading does not contain articles but the first sentence of the section does.

XII Policy on Marine Area of Surrounding Islands

***The** policy on **the** marine area of **the** surrounding islands has recently been . . .*

2.7 Exercises

A. Select the , a , an , or zero (no article) for each noun instance in this extract.

It was important to contact employees from the a an zero *SME in the region to see whether* the a an zero *theory was correct that these workers were not getting the training opportunities that the workers of larger corporations enjoyed. Contact was made first of all by* the a an zero *email, and then three visits were made to* the a an zero *chosen company to conduct* the a an zero *formal interviews.*

B. Circle the article errors made in this piece of writing.

Most previous investigations have been based on non-Chinese students lacking Chinese cultural values. Chinese learners have been greatly influenced by mainstream Chinese culture in their perception and behaviours when participating in the communication inside and outside classroom. 'The Chinese learner' is characterized as being reticent in the class. Wen and Clément (2003) explain that a Chinese students are influenced by classic Confucianism, in particular examination-oriented learning, shaping their understanding and way of the learning.

C. Some of these nouns require a definite article ('the'). Insert this article in the space provided for those that do.

_____ student attendance has dropped to 78% in the past three months at the college.

In _____ case of an attack from another network user, three recommendations are given.

_____ quality of the products was also much higher.

It is possible that _____ author overlooked this peripheral region.

3
PRONOUNS AND QUANTIFIERS

Focus on . . . Pronouns

Gender

Quantifiers

This chapter begins by explaining how a writer should approach gender reference. It then looks at plural and possessive pronouns and how they can be effectively employed. Quantity phrases are explored by identifying those that should be used with singular nouns and verbs and those with plural. 'Of' phrases are introduced along with the relationship between indefinite articles and words of quantity. Then, two sets of quantifiers that always prove troublesome are examined.

Background / 3.1 gender / 3.2 singular and plural quantifiers / 3.3 'of' phrases / 3.4 few and little / 3.5 every and all / 3.6 other and another / 3.7 Exercises

Featured errors in 3:

a few (3.4)	either (3.2)	number of (3.2)
a little (3.4)	every (3.5)	one (3.2)
all (3.5)	he (3.1)	other (3.6)
another (3.6)	it (3.1)	several (3.2)
both (3.2)	its (3.1)	some (3.3)
do not (3.5)	more (3.2)	they (3.1)
each (3.2)	not (3.5)	various (3.2)

BACKGROUND: Sometimes nouns can be replaced by pronouns in a sentence, especially when they are the subject of the sentence. Pronouns are used instead of nouns to indicate someone or something already mentioned or known. The following are personal pronouns:

I   you   he   she   it   we   they

The personal pronouns above are used for the subject of the sentence, but there are others that are objects.

me   you   him   her   it   us   them

These pronouns are often used in academic writing for self-assessment and presenting interview findings but not generally for standard essay writing; fortunately, institutions and writers are beginning to see the benefits of the active voice (see 5.8) and employing the pronoun 'we', where appropriate, to represent themselves (often a single author).

We began by assessing how the device could be used in other fields.

Some scientific fields do advise against using the personal pronoun 'we' when the process is more important than the researcher. One simple way of avoiding the personal pronoun is to reference the work or the topic instead.

We review the three models that have been developed so far.

The paper reviews the three models that have been developed so far.

We also discovered that these changes occur almost immediately.

The findings revealed that these changes occur almost immediately.

Another way is to employ the passive voice (see 5.8); however, constant use can lead to a rather detached style and long-winded sentences (see 13.6).

Possessive pronouns include his, her/hers, its, our/ours, and their/theirs.

One issue here is the choice between 'there', 'they're', and the possessive pronoun 'their'. The following explains the difference.

'There' relates to a place: *It is also unusual to find complete specimens **there**.*

'Their' is the possessive form: *This is true of **their** earlier policy proposals.*

'They're' is a contracted form of 'they are' but should be avoided in academic writing unless it is a direct quote: *'I think **they're** unlikely to get permission for this.'*

* * *

A quantifier is a word or phrase that is used with a noun to show quantity. It can describe how many or how much of something there is. The key requirement when using quantifiers is to ensure that the noun and the verb match the term being used.

Both systems are *used by schools in the region.*

Every machine is *checked carefully before being operated.*

REVEALED: 3.1 – *How to reference gender correctly*

Many writers fail to realize that 'they' can refer to a single person. It can be used when a singular countable noun is representing a typical example of its kind or type. 'They' has the effect of keeping the gender neutral and avoids the awkward use of 'he/she' (this is especially useful when there are many references to he/she and his/her in a paragraph).

This next example is referring to a manager in general, i.e., any manager and not a particular person, so keeping the gender neutral is important.

*A manager must ensure that **he** has control in these situations.* ✘

*A manager must ensure that **they** have control in these situations.* ✔

'They' is still a plural pronoun though, which means it must take a plural noun ('have' in the example above).

Some English grammar guides suggest that 'they' for an individual is unsuitable for academic English and that a plural noun should be used instead, and that will naturally also take 'they'.

*Managers must ensure that **they** have control in these situations.*

But there are times when a singular noun is more appropriate. Here only one fund manager is needed so a plural noun would not sound right.

*"We needed to find **a fund manager** who has experience in this area so **they** will be able to advise us before the meeting," revealed Interviewee C.*

A writer who is discussing an individual may wish to keep the gender hidden. Again 'they/their' is an option for this.

*Initially, **they** trained to be a doctor but then moved into medical law.*

Equally, there may be a generic reference to the noun clearly implying one individual where the definite article and singular noun is suitable.

If the driver presses their device quick enough, they will be able to regain control with minimal consequences.

Without the use of this plural pronoun, the writer would be forced to write this:

If the driver presses his/her device quick enough, he/she will be able to regain control with minimal consequences.

Which style do you prefer?

* * *

'He' should be avoided unless the individual is known to be a man; 'it' should not be used to refer to people.

In this example a specific individual is being described, and that individual is a man, so 'he' is fine.

*The second interviewee was from Brand International, and **he** had worked for the company for 15 years.*

Naturally, companies and inanimate objects can be referred to by 'it'.

*A firm can maximize **its** potential by recruiting from this talent pool.*

But singular and plural errors need to be avoided.

Firms can maximize its potential by recruiting from this talent pool. ✘
*Firms can maximize **their** potential by recruiting from this talent pool.* ✔

This scheme has economic motivations because they highlight those areas where money could be saved and investment increased. ✘
*This scheme has economic motivations because **it** highlights those areas where money could be saved and investment increased.* ✔

A pronoun can be employed to prevent repetition in a sentence (see also 13.4) and to avoid possessive phrases (as shown below.) In the second example, the writer has used the possessive pronoun 'their' to avoid repeating the noun 'students'.

*The objectives of the program are designed for students to seize opportunities to speak English and improve **students'** confidence.*

*The objectives of the program are designed for students to seize opportunities to speak English and improve **their** confidence.* (See 3B.)

REVEALED: 3.2 – *Which quantifiers take singular verb forms and nouns and which ones take plural*

Quantifiers come before the noun and modify it. When these words are the subject of the sentence, it is sometimes difficult to know whether to use a singular or a plural verb. Some take singular, some plural, and others both.

One of these problematic quantifiers is 'each'. This next sentence represents a typical dilemma faced by a writer.

Each of the team members were/was asked to fill in the questionnaire.

'Each' (meaning each one) should be used with a singular verb form.

*Each of the team members **was** asked to fill in the questionnaire.*

When a noun immediately follows this quantifier, it should be in the singular form.

*During the process, **each actor** wants to maximize earnings, but **each is** constrained by the other since interdependent relationships have built up.*

* * *

'Either' (meaning either one or the other) should be used with a singular noun and a singular verb.

*Either **methods are** appropriate for this type of research.* ✘
*Either **method is** appropriate for this type of research.* ✔

As is also true of 'each', confusion normally arises when an 'of' phrase is used, because then a plural noun is needed. Note that the verb remains singular though.

> *Either of the methods **are** appropriate for this type of research.* ✘
>
> *Either of the methods **is** appropriate for this type of research.* ✔

▶ RELATED ERRORS:

There are a number of other quantifiers that cause problems for writers. Those that produce the most errors are surprisingly the ones that logically imply a plural situation.

both: plural noun and plural verb

> *Both **party** give high priority to these issues.* ✘
>
> *Both **parties** give high priority to these issues.* ✔

> *The information is exchanged in both **direction**.* ✘
>
> *The information is exchanged in both **directions**.* ✔

> *Both **has** the same motives for boycotting the event.* ✘
>
> *Both **have** the same motives for boycotting the event.* ✔

The term '*Both two*' should be avoided.

> *Both **two** studies are addressed next.* ✘

* * *

several: plural noun and plural verb

> *There are several **reason** why this had an impact.* ✘
>
> *There are several **reasons** why this had an impact.* ✔

> *Several **has** expressed a desire to be part of the study* ✘
>
> *Several **have** expressed a desire to be part of the study.* ✔

* * *

various: plural noun and plural verb

> *Various **step** need to be taken before the project can begin.* ✘
>
> *Various **steps** need to be taken before the project can begin.* ✔

 This next quantifier implies singular but actually takes a plural noun when used in an 'of' phrase (the same as 'each' and 'either' above).

> *One of the **problem** is that they cannot test the machine beforehand.* ✘
>
> *One of the **problems** is that they cannot test the machine beforehand.* ✔

* * *

A quantity phrase that tends to catch writers out is 'a number of' and 'the number of'. The expressions require different verb forms.

> *A number of options **are** available to these prospective entrepreneurs.* (plural verb)
>
> *The number of people **is** smaller for this task.* (singular verb)

But the phrase should not be used with 'more'.

> *More **number of problems** will likely occur if this is not changed.* ✘
>
> *More **problems** will likely occur if this is not changed.* ✔

REVEALED: 3.3 – *How an 'of' phrase can change the meaning of the sentence*

As seen above, words of quantity can be followed by 'of'; however, writers often forget to place an article between the term and the noun.

> *Some of theories concentrate on the supply chain, including . . .* ✘
>
> ***Some of the theories** concentrate on the supply chain, including . . .* ✔

There is an apparent choice between leaving out 'of the' and using it, but the two styles can actually have different meanings.

most people/most of the people

By including the 'of' phrase, the sentence takes on a specific meaning.

> ***Most of the people*** *think this is a good idea*. (definite: a specific group of people)
>
> ***Most people*** *think this is a good idea*. (indefinite: people in general)
>
> ***All of the companies*** *will struggle under these financial constraints*. (definite: a specific group of companies)
>
> ***All companies*** *will struggle under these financial constraints*. (indefinite: companies in general)

REVEALED: 3.4 – *The difference between few/little and a few/a little*

Sometimes, two similar-looking phrases can have very different meanings. The addition of 'a' to the quantity words 'few' and 'little' has implications and in fact produces the opposite effect.

few: almost none

> *They can take **few** positives from the findings*. (negative result)

This means 'almost none' and does not represent a good outcome.

a few: some

> *They can take **a few** positives from the findings*. (positive result)

This means 'some', so the findings are considered to have been a reasonable success.

The writer in this next example wished to express that it was very likely that no rain would fall on the field trip day; however, the sentence in fact implies that there is a possibility that some rain would fall.

> *There was a little chance that rain would fall because of the time of year and location, and so this was one of the reasons for choosing this particular date.*

To produce the desired effect that there was no real chance of the event happening (that rain would fall), 'little' is required, not 'a little'.

There was little chance that rain would fall . . .

Here is another example to clarify the point.

*There was **little** moisture left in the bottle. (almost none)*

*There was **a little** moisture left in the bottle. (some)*

If the sentence has a negative implication (in the case below *losing accuracy*), then the positive/negative meanings of 'few'/'little', 'a few'/'a little' are reversed.

*There was **little** loss of accuracy here.* (almost none: positive outcome)

*There was **a little** loss of accuracy here.* (some: negative outcome)

(See 16.7 for information on 'fewer' and 'less'.)

REVEALED: 3.5 *– How to use 'every' and 'all'*

If a plural noun is chosen, then only certain quantifiers can precede it. Two quantifiers that consistently prove troublesome are 'every' and 'all'. The actual meaning is not the issue in the first example below, because either of the quantifiers can be employed; the issue is the agreement between the quantifier and the noun.

'Every' is used with singular nouns.

'All' is used with plural nouns and uncountable nouns.

Every respondents gave positive feedback on question six. ✗

Every respondent gave positive feedback on question six. ✔ OR

All respondents gave positive feedback on question six. ✔

Every evidence must be presented at this time. ✗

All evidence must be presented at this time. ✔

A plural noun has been used in this next example, so 'all' is required. A singular noun would have required 'every'.

This was so that every models could be evaluated. ✗

This was so that all models could be evaluated. ✔

Sometimes 'all' is used to begin a sentence that has a negative construction (do not).

All of the subjects do not exercise regularly. ✘

A better way is to begin with 'none of the' and to remove the verb.

None *of the subjects exercises regularly.* ✔

Another issue occurs when the writer actually means 'only some'. For this, 'not all' can be used.

All of the subjects do not have a family history of this. ✘

Not all of the subjects *have a family history of this.* ✔

For negation, 'any', not 'all', should be used to mean none. In the sentence below, 'all' would imply that it still worked on some of the subjects.

This did not work for all of the subjects. (It worked for some of them.)

This did not work for any of the subjects. (It worked for none of them.)

REVEALED: 3.6 – *When to use 'other' and 'another'*

Two other terms that writers use incorrectly are 'another' and 'other'. 'Another' is used with a singular countable noun; 'other' takes a plural or uncountable noun. The following mistake should be familiar to most writers.

Other issue is related to the lack of funding from public sources. ✘

Another issue *is related to the lack of funding from public sources.* ✔

If the writer wanted to state that there were a few issues, then the sentence would begin: ***Other issues are*** related to . . .

Another evidence relates to wider cultural trends. ✘

Other *evidence relates to wider cultural trends.* ✔

In the example above, the uncountable noun 'evidence' is used, so 'other' is required. If the writer wants to differentiate among the evidence, then a quantity term such as 'piece of' can be used with 'another': ***Another piece of evidence*** *relates* . . . (See also 1.1.)

For countable nouns, think of the terms in the following way:

another: singular (one other; a further)

other: plural (some other; further)

 When using a number to state how many 'other' of something there are, write the number first.

Other two studies have discussed the implications of this measure. ✗
***Two other** studies have discussed the implications of this measure.* ✔

(See also 16.2.)

3.7 Exercises

A. Some (but not all) of these sentences contain errors. Rewrite the ones that contain errors in the spaces below.

A manager must ensure that he listens to his staff at all times.

Other issue is that the software took too long to load.

There have been few problems with attendance, so they decided to warn the pupils.

Every employee is entitled to a break every two hours.

We can then change this into another formats.

_____

_____

_____

_____

B. Fill in the gaps with quantifier words. There may be a choice for some of them.

one   both   some   all   less   fewer

_____ of the models failed to produce satisfactory results, so we decided to create our own.

It is important to make sure that with each draft _____ mistakes are made.

_____ of the evidence points to the fact that these policies have failed to boost the economy.

There is _____ risk involved, so these investors might be tempted.

This only worked for _____ of the regions, as revealed in Table 4.

There was _____ participant without knowledge of the procedure.

4
SUBJECT AND VERB

Focus on ... Subject-verb agreement

Collective nouns

Questions

This chapter explains the subject-verb agreement rule for sentences. It gives situations in which it is difficult to recognize the subject in a sentence and then moves on to problems relating to collective nouns. The chapter also explores how the structure of questions is different from that of statements.

Background / 4.1 identifying the subject / 4.2 repeating the subject / 4.3 collective nouns / 4.4 questions and statements / 4.5 Exercises

Featured errors in 4:

can (4.4)	it (4.2)
company (4.3)	purpose (4.1)
group (4.3)	role (4.1)
he (4.2)	they (4.2)
how (4.4)	what (4.4)
issues (4.1)	would (4.4)

BACKGROUND: To ensure that the correct verb form is chosen for a sentence, it is necessary to identify the subject.

The main purpose of the three models was to see how the population affected the resources of the region.

Subject-verb agreement means that the main verb of the sentence matches the subject, i.e., that both are singular or both plural. The subject comes before the verb when making statements. In the example above, the subject is 'The main purpose (of the three models)' and the verb is 'was'. Both of these are singular, so the sentence has subject-verb agreement.

REVEALED: 4.1 – *How to identify the subject in a sentence and consequently select the correct verb form*

Confusion occurs when there is extra information between the subject and the verb. The example above is a good example of this, because 'three models' sits between the subject and the verb and could be a source of confusion.

*The main purpose of the three models **were** to see how the population affected the resources of the region.* ✗

The writer of the sentence above has been influenced by the plural noun phrase 'three models' and used a plural form of the verb ('were') to match it. But if it is not the subject of the sentence, it should not affect the verb form. Here is another example:

*The role of consultants in this field **have** changed considerably.* ✗

'Consultants' is not the subject of the sentence; the singular noun 'role' forms the subject, so a singular verb is required.

*The **role** of consultants in this field **has** changed considerably.* ✔

Here is an example in which a singular noun ('project manager') has confused things. The subject is in fact plural ('key issues') and therefore the verb should be as well.

*The key issues for the project manager **is** divided into four areas (see Table 11).* ✗

*The key issues for the project manager **are** divided into four areas (see Table 11).* ✔

REVEALED: 4.2 – *When the subject is mistakenly repeated in a sentence*

Sometimes a pronoun that repeats the subject is unnecessarily added. In all these examples the subject has already been named and so does not require a second reference to it.

Herbert Jones, one of Leung's students, **he** *stated that people's perceptions were heavily involved in this.* ✘

Herbert Jones, one of Leung's students, stated that people's perceptions were heavily involved in this. ✔

The study **it** *aimed to fill in the gaps left by previous research on this topic.* ✘

The study aimed to fill in the gaps left by previous research on this topic. ✔

. . . and the problems **they** *were increased by the poor attitude of the workers.* ✘

. . . and the problems were increased by the poor attitude of the workers. ✔

REVEALED: 4.3 – *How to match the verb to a collective noun*

Using the correct verb form for collective nouns (e.g., company, family, firm, group, public, school, society, team) is not always straightforward. Sometimes these nouns appear to be correct with a singular verb and a plural verb.

The government has pledged to support these local schemes in the future.

The government have been struggling to come to an agreement on this matter.

Usually collective nouns take the singular form because they are considered a unit—a single entity.

The **committee is** *meeting this Friday to discuss the issue.*

But if the members of the group are not acting together but rather as individuals, a plural verb form can be used.

The **committee have** *different opinions on this matter.*

Note the contexts of the two sentences above. The first is referring to a meeting that the committee as a group will attend; the second is referring to divided opinions in the committee, and therefore the group has been viewed as comprising different parts.

In these next examples, the singular verb form is preferred because the collective nouns are clearly acting as one.

The company **are** moving its headquarters to Shanghai in November. ✘

The company **is** moving its headquarters to Shanghai in November. ✔

The first group **have** been given a marking scheme to evaluate. ✘

The first group **has** been given a marking scheme to evaluate. ✔

REVEALED: 4.4 *– The difference between questions and statements and the various forms that questions can take*

The subject normally comes before the verb, but in sentences that are questions the verb is written before the subject.

Are the figures reliable?

If the question above is rewritten as a statement, the subject ('the figures') would come before the verb ('are').

The figures are reliable.

Writers sometimes make statements when they actually want to ask questions.

They can adapt to the firm's philosophy? ✘

This is not a question; it is a statement. To make it a question, the subject and verb (in this case the modal verb 'can') have to change places.

Can they adapt to the firm's philosophy? ✔

Equally, some statements are turned into questions by mistake.

We will now look at why **is this** the case. ✘

This is supposed to be a statement and therefore should be written as follows:

We will now look at why **this is** the case. ✔

(See also interrogative statements in 6.4.)

Questions contain auxiliary verbs ('be', 'do', 'have') and/or modal verbs ('will', 'would', 'can', 'could', etc.). Sometimes these verbs are missed out completely.

You change anything about the current system? ✗

__Would you__ change anything about the current system? ✔

Interrogative words can also be used in questions. They are placed at the start of the question:

how, what, where, why, when, which, who, whose

Who is the new CEO of the company?

Another mistake is to correctly place the interrogative word at the beginning of the question but put the auxiliary verb or the modal after the subject or at the end.

What __managers can__ do to overcome this barrier? ✗

What __can managers__ do to overcome this barrier? ✔

__Who__ the new CEO of the company __is__? ✗

__Who is__ the new CEO of the company? ✔

'How' questions tend to be mistakenly written without a modal or auxiliary.

__How to__ change this with limited support? ✗

There are a number of solutions to this particular mistake.

How __can this be__ changed with limited support? ✔

How __can we__ change this with limited support? ✔

How __do we__ change this with limited support? ✔

▷ RELATED ERRORS:

Interrogative words have very specific meanings and perform different roles in questions. Two that require extra attention are 'how' and 'what'.

how: in what way; by what means

what: to what extent; used to ask about the identity, nature, or value of something

What will this change the performance of the workers? ✘

How will this change the performance of the workers? ✔

How are the effects on the speaking abilities of the students? ✘

What are the effects on the speaking abilities of the students? ✔

4.5 Exercises

A. Identify the subject and then select the appropriate verb form.

The assistance provided to these people is/are important because it is the only support available to them.

Networking in groups is/are more effective than walking around as an individual is.

Educating these groups prevent/prevents them from getting involved in crime and anti-social behaviour.

Workers who had enrolled in the scheme was/were more likely to have a positive attitude towards their company.

Most of the students' perceived speaking improvements is/are related to presentation skills.

B. Add a question mark to the sentences you think are questions and a full stop to those that are statements.

We will also ask whether they have noticed an improvement in the past six months

They can change this at any point during the process

The teacher must decide if this is acceptable behaviour

How can this system be changed to suit every department

How these reports are assessed is another talking point

What relationships can be formed when these two areas combine

5
VERBS AND TENSES

Focus on . . . The verb 'to be'

        Verbals (infinitive, –ing form, participles)

        Tense

        Voice (active and passive)

The chapter begins with an examination of the forms of the verb 'to be'. Verbals are introduced and categorized by their various forms and uses. The relationship between participles and irregular verbs is then assessed. When to employ the different tenses precedes a discussion about the active and the passive voices.

Background / 5.1 to be / 5.2 being and been / 5.3 introduction to verbals / 5.4 infinitive 'to' / 5.5 when to use –*ing* / 5.6 past participle use / 5.7 tense selection / 5.8 passive vs. active voice / 5.9 Exercises

Featured errors in 5:

afford (5.4)	discuss (5.3)	underwent (5.6)
after (5.5)	fail (5.4)	watch (5.4)
allow (5.4)	following (5.7)	with (5.2)
as (5.2)	in (5.5)	withdrew (5.6)
been (5.2)	instruct (5.4)	worth considering (5.5)
began (5.6)	plan (5.4)	worth mentioning (5.5)
being (5.2)	previous (5.7)	
chose (5.6)	recommend (5.3)	
convince (5.4)	shake (5.6)	
despite (5.5)	suggest (5.3)	

BACKGROUND: The verb 'to be' is an irregular verb and unique in its construction. It is so common in English that becoming familiar with its various forms is vital.

to be   1. to exist or live   2. to take place; to occur
3. having a specified state or role

present participle: **being**   past participle: **been**

Simple past		Past perfect		Past progressive	
I	**was**	I	**had been**	I	**was being**
it/she/he	**was**	it/she/he	**had been**	it/she/he	**was being**
we/they	**were**	we/they	**had been**	we/they	**were being**

Simple present		Present perfect		Present progressive	
I	**am**	I	**have been**	I	**am being**
it/she/he	**is**	it/she/he	**has been**	it/she/he	**is being**
we/they	**are**	we/they	**have been**	we/they	**are being**

Simple future		Future perfect		Future progressive	
I	**will be**	I	**will have been**	I	**will be being**
it/she/he	**will be**	it/she/he	**will have been**	it/she/he	**will be being**
we/they	**will be**	we/they	**will have been**	we/they	**will be being**

REVEALED: 5.1 – *When 'to be' is included in error or mistakenly left out*

The needless insertion of the simple present form ('is', 'are') is one of the most common errors associated with the verb 'to be'.

*This **is** depends on a number of factors, and these have been categorized in Figure 6.* ✗

This depends on a number of factors, and these have been categorized in Figure 6. ✔

*These books **are** recorded all the incidents that took place in the first term.* ✗

These books recorded all the incidents that took place in the first term. ✔

In the last example the progressive tense could have been used alongside 'are':

These books are recording all the incidents that take place in the first term.

The verb 'to be' is used alongside participles (see 5.3–5.6 and 8.3) and in passive writing (see 5.8). Missing out the verb is a frequent error when forming the passive voice. In these next examples the writer has overlooked it.

Over 5,000 participants involved in the survey. ✘

*Over 5,000 participants **were** involved in the survey.* ✔

The experiment carried out by researchers at the local college. ✘

*The experiment **was** carried out by researchers at the local college.* ✔

REVEALED: 5.2 – *When to use 'being' and when to use 'been'*

The verb form 'being' is the present participle of the verb and is used for the present progressive tense, which involves an ongoing action.

*We will now look at how they are **been** affected.* ✘

*We will now look at how they are **being** affected.* ✔

The form 'been' is the past participle and is always found after the verb 'to have'.

*I **have been** busy choosing a methodology for my research.*

Often the two are confused.

*These models have **being** used before in similar studies.* ✘

*These models have **been** used before in similar studies.* ✔

The form to use after a preposition is 'being' (see 5.5). This is demonstrated in the following example that contains the preposition 'with':

*There may be some people who agree to be interviewed but are not happy **with** been audio recorded.* ✘

*There may be some people who agree to be interviewed but are not happy **with** being audio recorded.* ✔

It is often difficult to know when to employ the various forms of the verb 'to be', but the preposition rule is useful to know. Another situation that offers some clarity is when writing about a particular point in time.

'Has been' is used to describe something that happened in the past, but the actual time of the event is not important. It may be linked with something continuing today. There is some overlap between 'was' and 'has been', but the error is made when a particular point in time is used. A date in the past usually means that the present perfect ('has been') cannot be applied.

> In 2009 a new system **has been** created to make the task easier. ✘
>
> In 2009 a new system **was** created to make the task easier. ✔

The exceptions to this are a particular date being used with 'since' to show that the event is still continuing today and when the current year is stated.

> The chief executive of the company (who since 2009 **was** Dr Leung) was also unavailable for comment. ✘
>
> The chief executive of the company (who since 2009 **has been** Dr Leung) was also unavailable for comment. ✔
>
> Fortunately, 2016 **has been** different because of the introduction of more stringent safety standards.

*   *   *

In the next examples, the writers have failed to construct the present perfect correctly.

> Many results **have obtained** for this particular subgroup. ✘
>
> Many results **have been obtained** for this particular subgroup. ✔

> Several systems **have successfully** used to extract the data. ✘
>
> Several systems **have been successfully** used to extract the data. ✔

▮➤ RELATED ERRORS:

The simple present form 'is' tends to be confused with 'as'. This mistake can occur in phrases where things are being defined, described, or regarded, as these examples demonstrate:

> They define a pilot study **is** an initial test of the ideas and … ✘
>
> They define a pilot study **as** an initial test of the ideas and … ✔

> They view this **is** a setback in the relations between the two countries. ✘
>
> They view this **as** a setback in the relations between the two countries. ✔

REVEALED: 5.3 – *The function of verbals and verbs that are followed by the -ing form*

Verbals represent a challenging area for the writer of English in that, although they are derived from verbs, they function as nouns, adjectives, or adverbs in a sentence.

Three types are recognized.

Gerunds are verb forms that end in *–ing* and act like nouns.

> ***Comparing*** *the three systems allowed us to select the best one for this region.*

Infinitives are verb forms that are usually preceded by 'to' and that act like nouns, adjectives, or adverbs.

> *Barnes (2001) collected them* ***to investigate*** *why this happens so frequently.*

Participles are verb forms that usually end in *–ing* or *–ed* and that act like adjectives.

> *This is vital in a* ***developing*** *industry.*
>
> *A* ***completed*** *study has yet to be achieved by this group.*

These labels are useful to know, but at the practical level the dilemma a writer will often face is whether to use the *–ing* form or 'to + verb'. It is certainly a problem when there is already a main verb in the sentence and the writer is trying to determine what verbal form should come after it.

> *I anticipate to find/I anticipate finding further errors in the data.*

The answer is that some main verbs are followed by *–ing* and some are followed by 'to + verb'—and these just have to be learnt; for instance, 'anticipate' is always followed by the *–ing* form.

> *I anticipate* ***finding*** *further errors in the data.*

The *–ing* form is also used after 'admit'. If another verb form follows the verb to 'admit', it must end in *–ing*.

> *They* ***admit*** *taking a risk with this proposal.*

|➤ RELATED ERRORS:

The following is a selection of examples where the wrong choice has been made; these verbs all require the *–ing* form after them.

> They also **discussed to put** the project back one month. ✗
>
> They also **discussed putting** the project back one month. ✔
>
> The paper **recommended to invest** in this market. ✗
>
> The paper **recommended investing** in this market. ✔
>
> My supervisor **suggested to find** a better logo. ✗
>
> My supervisor **suggested finding** a better logo. ✔

These verbs are also always followed by the *–ing* form (e.g., *They also **advise seeing** a specialist*):

advise	deny	miss	resist
appreciate	dislike	postpone	risk
avoid	enjoy	practice	stop
consider	finish	recall	tolerate
delay	keep	resent	understand

Verbs that relate to causation, i.e., someone or something causing something else to happen, can be followed by the 'to + verb' form if an object (noun or pronoun) is present. 'Advise' is one such verb. (See also 5.4.)

We advise moving this to section four.   OR

We advise them to move this to section four.

REVEALED: 5.4 – *The verbs that are followed by the infinitive ('to + verb') form and the verbs that need an actor*

As with the *–ing* form, there are some verbs that have to be followed by the infinitive 'to + verb' form.

The following is a selection of examples where the wrong choice has been made. These sentences all require the infinitive form after the main verb.

> *They could not afford **ignoring** the advice.* ✘
>
> *They could not afford **to ignore** the advice.* ✔
>
> *It was surprising that they failed **noticing** what was happening around them* ✘
>
> *It was surprising that they failed **to notice** what was happening around them.* ✔
>
> *We plan **working** on this for the next few months.* ✘
>
> *We plan **to work** on this for the next few months.* ✔

Here are some more verbs that are followed by the 'to + verb' form (e.g., *Twenty employees agreed to participate in the research*):

agree	claim	hope	offer	seem
appear	decide	intend	prepare	struggle
arrange	demand	learn	pretend	threaten
ask	deserve	manage	promise	wait
attempt	expect	mean	propose	want
care	hesitate	need	refuse	wish

 Some verbs can take either the infinitive or the *–ing* form with no real change in meaning. These include:

> begin, continue, forget, like, prefer, regret, remember, start, try

*Fifty percent said they will continue **to work** hard.*

*Fifty percent said they will continue **working** hard.*

*The new officer must start **to make** decisions.*

*The new officer must start **making** decisions.*

Some can take either but with a change in meaning.

> *One participant said that he always stopped to buy a coffee.*
>
> *Many of the participants revealed that they had stopped buying coffee.*

Another situation in which the infinitive form should be used is after participles that are acting as adjectives.

> *They were **relieved to see** progress was finally being made.*
>
> *It was **interesting to hear** their views on these treatments.*

Notice how the verb cannot change when preceded by 'to'; it must retain the simple or dictionary form. These next examples show the writer being influenced by tense.

> *The company tried **to changed** their logo last year to reflect their new image.* ✘
>
> *The company tried **to change** their logo last year to reflect their new image.* ✔

> *They were always looking for opportunities **to speaking** the language outside of the classroom.* ✘
>
> *They were always looking for opportunities **to speak** the language outside of the classroom.* ✔

▷ RELATED ERRORS:

Sometimes the infinitive form is used without the 'to'.

> *We should see the resources **improve** in the next few years.*

This is known as the base form or the bare infinitive. Besides being used for the present tense and with modals (see Chapter 6), it is found after the object of verbs that involve seeing or hearing (e.g., look, feel, hear, notice, watch, see, smell, observe).

> *The pupils could watch their peers **to compete** and then learn from them.* ✘
>
> *The pupils could watch their peers **compete** and then learn from them.* ✔

It is also found after objects when the main verb is 'have', 'make', and 'let'.

> *My tutor made me **read** through the chapter again.*

*   *   *

The main verb in a sentence cannot always be directly followed by another verb form. Some verbs require an actor (a pronoun or a noun) between them and the verbal.

A verb that always causes problems is 'to allow'.

This will allow to calculate the other values. ✘

Another word is needed in between (either a pronoun or a noun).

*This will allow **us/them/the engineer** to calculate the other values.* ✔

If pronouns have to be avoided, one option is to make the sentence passive.

This will allow the other values to be calculated.

The infinitive ('to + verb') can immediately follow 'allow' if the verb is in the past participle form and alongside the verb 'to be'. Compare the following:

In this first example an actor is required (in brackets).

*We allowed (**the patients in groups 1 and 2**) to apply this liberally.*

But in this next example 'allowed' can be followed by the infinitive.

Patients in groups 1 and 2 were allowed to apply this liberally.

▷ RELATED ERRORS:

Other verbs that usually require an actor in the active voice include:

advise, convince, enable, encourage, instruct, and permit

The researcher will then instruct to apply the cream. ✘
*The researcher will then instruct **the patient** to apply the cream.* ✔

We can then convince to adopt these measures. ✘
*We can then convince **the staff** to adopt these measures.* ✔

REVEALED: 5.5 – *Other situations where the –ing form should be used but is overlooked*

One function of the *–ing* form is to create the progressive tense.

*They are **trying** to complete the project before the new guidelines come into force.*

As the present participle, it acts like an adjective in these two examples.

*The second report **is interesting** because it details the reforms that have yet to take place.*

*This is an **interesting aspect** of the discussion for a number of reasons.*

As mentioned earlier, the *–ing* form must be used after a preposition.

*There is little benefit **in keep** the original component.* ✘

*There is little benefit **in keeping** the original component.* ✔

*Despite the schools **are** rural, the facilities were better than expected.* ✘

*Despite the schools **being** rural, the facilities were better than expected.* ✔

*After **review** the current situation, three proposals will be drawn up.* ✘

*After **reviewing** the current situation, three proposals will be drawn up.* ✔

⊳ RELATED ERRORS:

The following error is commonly made:

*It is **worth to mention** that only those participants that had experience in this area were invited back for interview.* ✘

*It is **worth mentioning** that only those participants that had experience in this area were invited back for interview.* ✔

'Worth' is an adjective but it acts a bit like a preposition in this phrase (it has been called a marginal preposition). It should therefore be followed by the *–ing* form and not the infinitive.

Note also that '**worth to consider**' should be written '**worth considering**'.

* * *

Mistakes are also made when a gerund phrase or present participle phrase begins a sentence. These sentence starters require the first word to be in the *–ing* form.

> **Compare** *the two frameworks led to an insight into which factors should remain.* ✘
>
> **Comparing** *the two frameworks led to an insight into which factors should remain.* ✔
>
> **Refer** *primarily to the examination system, Morgan highlighted the strong organization of the schools in the country.* ✘
>
> **Referring** *primarily to the examination system, Morgan highlighted the strong organization of the schools in the country.* ✔

Below is another example of the base form (or infinitive without the 'to') being used instead of the *–ing* form. The writer in this example is suggesting some actions that could be carried out. Although an infinitive ('To clarify' . . .) can also start a sentence in this way, the gerund is the preferred option.

> **Clarify** *and* **verify** *existing discourse is also useful at this stage.* ✘
>
> **Clarifying** *and* **verifying** *existing discourse is also useful at this stage.* ✔

REVEALED: 5.6 *– When the past participle should be employed and errors to look out for*

There are two errors of note when it comes to participles. The first relates to the fact that the past participle form of irregular verbs can be different from the past tense form.

irregular verb: **to grow**   past tense: **grew**   past participle: **grown**

When an auxiliary verb form such as 'has/have' or 'was/were' is used, then the past participle must follow. (Also see the Appendix.)

> *It* **grew** *in the final quarter of 2005.*
> *It has* **grown** *in the first quarter of the year.*
>
> *This* **became** *a problem when the class size increased.*
> *This has* **become** *an issue in the rural areas.*

The form of the verb is different in the second examples with the auxiliary verb ('has') present because 'to become' and 'to grow' are irregular verbs. Irregular verbs just need to be learnt. A list can be found in the Appendix. The following seem to cause particular problems though, and writers should certainly become familiar with them:

to begin   past tense: **began**   past participle: **begun**

> *The move towards this new technology **has now began**.* ✘
> *The move towards this new technology **has now begun**.* ✔

to choose   past tense: **chose**   past participle: **chosen**

> *These specific cells **were chose** from the original 200 samples.* ✘
> *These specific cells **were chosen** from the original 200 samples.* ✔

to shake   past tense: **shook**   past participle: **shaken**

> *The two bottles **were then shaked** for five minutes to allow the particles to mix.* ✘
> *The two bottles **were then shaken** for five minutes to allow the particles to mix.* ✔

to undergo   past tense: **underwent**   past participle: **undergone**

> *According to the criteria, the participants **had underwent** some kind of surgery in the past year.* ✘
> *According to the criteria, the participants **had undergone** some kind of surgery in the past year.* ✔

to withdraw   past tense: **withdrew**   past participle: **withdrawn**

> *These participants **had withdrew** so their details were deleted from the records.* ✘
> *These participants **had withdrawn** so their details were deleted from the records.* ✔

The second notable error relating to participles is forgetting to add 'd' when the past participles of regular verbs are being used like adjectives and are modifying a noun.

> *The **balance** diets were associated with the best overall scores.* ✘
> *The **balanced** diets were associated with the best overall scores.* ✔

> *There were a number of issues with the **estimate** recovery times* ✘
> *There were a number of issues with the **estimated** recovery times.* ✔

▶ RELATED ERRORS:

Similarly, when the past participle is employed after a linking verb such as 'to be', writers need to ensure the correct form is used.

> In this situation, the cash flow is **reduces** to an appropriate rate. ✗
>
> In this situation, the cash flow is **reduced** to an appropriate rate. ✔

* * *

Another source of confusion is auxiliary verbs ('to be' and 'to have') in the perfect and progressive tenses and which participle form to choose. (See also 8.3 for when to select a present and a past participle.)

> This **is changed** the way we think about energy usage in the home. ✗
>
> Two options are:
>
> This **is changing** the way we think about energy usage in the home. ✔
>
> This **has changed** the way we think about energy usage in the home. ✔

> They are looking at the way this **is implementing**. ✗
>
> Two options are:
>
> They are looking at the way this **is being implemented**. ✔
>
> They are looking at the way this **has been implemented**. ✔

REVEALED: 5.7 – *Which tense to employ at different stages of a paper*

Often writers are instructed to create their literature review in a certain tense. If the instruction is to write in the past tense, this does not mean that every verb should be written in the past tense; some writers think it does.

> In general terms, a mixed diet incorporating many different kinds of vegetable was essential to human health. Morgan analysed three types of . . . ✗

Using the past tense for the literature review means that reporting verbs (e.g., 'analysed' above) and any particular experiments or research are written and explained in the past tense. In the example above, a well-known fact is stated (that a mixed diet is essential), so the verb should be in the present tense ('is' essential to human health). If something is still true today or is a current event, then the past tense is inappropriate. Even if a particular tense is to be favoured, each verb should be assessed for appropriate usage. So past tense does not mean past tense for everything. (See also 15.3 for advice on which tense to use with dates.)

Here is another example to further illustrate the point. The reporting verb ('questioned') can be used in the past tense, but the other verbs in this tense imply that the information may not still be true today.

> Morgan (2011) **questioned** this because the United Nations' offices **were** situated in Geneva, Vienna, and Nairobi . . . the UN **was** an international organization founded in 1945. ✘

So, the present tense should be used.

> Morgan (2011) **questioned** this because the United Nations' offices **are** situated in Geneva, Vienna, and Nairobi . . . the UN **is** an international organization founded in 1945. ✔

Despite their evident meaning, tense is often misused when writers use 'previous', 'following', and 'next' when referring to chapters and sections.

> The previous chapter **looks** at the problems in rural areas and then **assesses** . . . ✘
>
> The previous chapter **looked** at the problems in rural areas and then **assessed** . . . ✔
>
> In the following section we **demonstrated** how this could be achieved. ✘
>
> In the following section we **demonstrate/will demonstrate** how this could be achieved. ✔

(See also 17.1.)

The example above reveals that reporting verbs can be in the present form or the future when referring to the content of an upcoming section.

> In this chapter, **I demonstrate** how the research fills the gap in the literature and how the nature of the topic affects the research process. **I also clarify** the challenges and ethical issues.
>
> In this chapter, **I will demonstrate** how the research fills the gap in the literature and how the nature of the topic affects the research process. **I will also clarify** the challenges and ethical issues.

* * *

When summarizing or concluding, the past tense is the natural choice.

*This study **employed** a mixed methods design to ensure that . . .*

The present perfect is also a suitable tense for this task.

*This paper **has argued** that product placement is less effective in the markets under study.*

REVEALED: 5.8 – *The differences between the active and the passive voice*

There are two types of voice that writers can use in English, the active and the passive. The subject performs the action in a sentence with an active voice.

We analysed the data to confirm this relationship.

The word order is altered to make the sentence passive.

The subject then goes from performing the action to being acted upon by the verb. Note how the original subject (we) no longer features in the passive voice sentence.

The data were analysed to confirm this relationship.

In the passive voice, a form of 'to be' (in this case 'were') is used and comes before the past participle ('analysed').

The passive voice is used when the writer wishes to remain neutral or does not want to explicitly reveal the person carrying out the action (even though it may be obvious).

The researcher interpreted the results incorrectly for the first stage. (active)

The results were interpreted incorrectly for the first stage. (passive, and no direct mention of the researcher)

A common error occurs when the writer tries to use both the active and the passive voice in a sentence with consecutive and linked actions.

*The scale was picked and **then analysed the differences**.* ✗

*The scale was picked and **then the differences were analysed**.* ✔

*The issue is clarified and then **discussed the effects on speaking ability**.* ✗

*The issue is clarified and then **the effects on speaking ability are discussed**.* ✔

> ❗ The passive voice is therefore used when the writer wishes to avoid the personal pronouns 'we' and 'I'. (See 3B.)
>
> *We changed this material to a breathable one.* (active with personal pronoun)
>
> *The material was changed to a breathable one.* (passive without personal pronoun)
>
> *We will analyse this further in the next chapter.* (active with personal pronoun)
>
> *This will be analysed further in the next chapter.* (passive without personal pronoun)

5.9 Exercises

A. Select the appropriate option for each of these sentences. Underneath each sentence explain why it is the correct choice.

There seems to be an issue with to extract / extract / extracting all the data from this program.

_____

They should let the students to think / think / thinking for themselves some of the time.

_____

They were allowed to change / change / changing their minds and select a different object if they were not happy.

_____

Despite this to increase / increase / increasing the budget, the project was too expensive to carry out.

_____

B. How many verb or verbal errors can you find in this passage?

Although three participants withdraw from the research, we had enough to beginning the experiment. Group A were all meant to underwent the full experiment, but time constraints meant that they had to chose between the partial and the full experiment. Whenever the liquid become too cloudy, the researcher asked an assistant to shaken the bottle, and when this happened the clock was stopped. _____

C. Rewrite the following sentences by either correcting the grammar or simplifying them.

The following diagram demonstrated these connections and labelled the stages.

_____

We designed the logo and then a presentation of the final product was given.

_____

This allowed to change the final design and submit their work on time.

_____

D. Change these active sentences into the passive voice and therefore omit the subject at the beginning of each sentence (i.e., we, the teacher . . .)

We tested the product the following week.

_____

The teacher asked the class to quieten down on a number of occasions.

_____

The researcher reduced the number of participants for the next stage.

_____

6
MODALS

Focus on . . . Modal verbs

The verb 'to do'

This chapter introduces modal verbs, reveals the specific rules to follow and demonstrates how modals influence other verb forms. The chapter also addresses the problems encountered when using the verb 'to do' and this verb's relationship with questions.

Background / 6.1 modal rules / 6.2 'would' or 'will'? / 6.3 using 'could' /
6.4 the verb 'to do' and questions and negatives / 6.5 Exercises

Featured errors in 6:

could (6.3)   should (6.4)
do (6.4)   would (6.2)
do not (6.4)

BACKGROUND: Modals are supporting verbs that show the likelihood or ability of something. They are followed by a main verb and give extra information relating to ability, possibility, necessity, or willingness.

will   would   can   could   may   might   must   should   shall

Will: This modal verb is used for a certain future prediction. By using 'will', the writer needs to be fairly certain it will happen! (See 6.2.)

*Funding **will** continue to decline in this sector because the government is now prioritizing soft skills.*

Would: This modal is usually used with 'if' to state that something will happen on the condition that something else does. (See 6.2.)

*This system **would** work if there was a dedicated support team.*

It can be used to express hope or justification.

*This activity **would** be able to teach the employees conflict resolution.*

'Would' is also the past tense of 'will'.

*The claim was that red **would** be a better colour for the logo than blue.*

Can: This modal is used for occasions when something is possible but may not happen.

*Devices **can** improve their performance over time.*

It is also used to show ability.

*The designers **can** change the material of the outer layer as well.*

Could, might: These modals also show possibility, but there is more doubt involved. (See 6.3.)

*It is unclear whether they **could** include developing countries in the index.*
*This **might** indicate a weakness in the original framework.*

'Could' is also the past tense of 'can'.

*We allowed two weeks so the participants **could** provide as much information as possible.*

Should: This modal is used for a good expectation that something will happen.

*This **should** alter the way in which product designers work in the industry.*

It is also used to note the limitations of a study and to make recommendations to others.

*Future interventions **should** take place at a neutral venue but with familiar staff present.*

May: One of the best ways to express degrees of certainty or to 'hedge' is to use a modal before the main verb. 'May' is often employed to add caution to a claim. It is possible, but there is some doubt.

*Adopting our proposed syllabus **may** give learning support tutors a more proactive role.*

'Shall' is a more formal version of 'will' and can mean 'do you want me to?'

'Must' is used for something that is necessary or essential.

REVEALED: 6.1 *– The main rules to follow for modal verbs*

Usually a verb is affected by tense and plurality.

*They have **remained** in the system despite leaving last year.*
*It **remains** in the system until the systems engineer removes the data.*

A useful rule to learn is that the verb that follows the modal will stay in its normal or base form regardless of the nature of the sentence.

*They will **remain** here until the teacher returns.*
*It should **remain** in the beaker only for a short period.*

If the modal is followed by 'be', then the verb that follows can be in a different form.

*They **could be spending** more money than they are earning.*

In this next example, even though the pronoun is singular ('she'), the verb is unaffected because of the modal (the main verb does not take an 's' as it normally would in the present tense: 'she moves').

> *She **should moves** around the class to ensure that every pupil is engaged in the task.* ✘
>
> *She **should move** around the class to ensure that every pupil is engaged in the task.* ✔

Normally the verb would be able to change for the pronoun 'she'/'he'.

> *She moves . . .   She moved . . .   She is moving . . .*

Some more example errors will help to illustrate the point.

> *A public accountant **must uses** ethical principles that serve as a guide in making decisions.* ✘
>
> *A public accountant **must use** ethical principles that serve as a guide in making decisions.* ✔

> *A loss of resources **could translates** into greater work engagement.* ✘
>
> *A loss of resources **could translate** into greater work engagement.* ✔

> The modal does not have to come directly before the verb to influence it.
>
> *Will this **shapes** the future policies of the government?* ✘
>
> *Will this **shape** the future policies of the government?* ✔

▷ RELATED ERRORS:

A common error is putting the verb in the past tense when it follows a modal. It is important to remember that the verb does not change its ending when alongside a modal.

> *This will **facilitated** the drug development process.* ✘
>
> *This will **facilitate** the drug development process.* ✔

Naturally, the *–ing* form cannot be used either.

*Then they could **facilitating** the lessons from a different location.* ✗

*Then they could **facilitate** the lessons from a different location.* ✔

REVEALED: 6.2 *– When to use 'would' and when to use 'will'*

Writers tend to use 'would' to inform the reader about what follows in their work or what they plan to discuss next. Because of its role in conditional sentences, it sounds to the reader as though this was not actually possible.

*We **would** choose this method for our study.* ✗

The reader is waiting for the second part of the sentence.

*We would choose this method for our study, **but our dataset is probably too small**.*

Instead, 'will' should inform the reader about what follows because it is a future event and 'will' represents future time.

*We **will** choose this material for reconstruction.*

*This **will** be covered in a later chapter.*

The only time that 'would' can be used in this context is for expressing hope or justification.

*The issue has been present in research up to now, but this study **would** be able to solve the problem.*

*This **would** be useful to teachers who struggle to prepare lessons in time.*

These examples further illustrate the error:

*This **would** be carried out in chapter three where the methodology is also discussed.* ✗

*This **will** be carried out in chapter three where the methodology is also discussed.* ✔

*We **would** address these issues when we evaluate the scheme.* ✗

*We **will** address these issues when we evaluate the scheme.* ✔

REVEALED: 6.3 – *When to use 'could' in a sentence*

'Could' is used to describe something that is possible in the present or the future but that may not happen for various reasons.

> We **could** interview these participants as well, but time constraints may prevent this from happening.

'Could' is also used to express alternatives or possible reasons for something.

> They **could** also look at cases where the problems were on a local scale.
>
> It **could** be that there was no power left in the device.

One area of difficulty is recognizing when the simple present is sufficient, without the need for modals or other tenses. Writers insert 'could' before the verb or 'could be' when there is actually no doubt involved in the sentence.

> We **could realize** that this is incomplete and therefore will add another layer to our design. ✗
>
> We **realize** that this is incomplete and therefore will add another layer to our design. ✔
>
> It **could be** normal to feel anxious in these situations, and many patients express this emotion on the initial visit. ✗
>
> It **is** normal to feel anxious in these situations, and many patients express this emotion on the initial visit. ✔

> 'Would be' is also possible here.
>
> It **would be** normal to feel anxious in these situations . . .

REVEALED: 6.4 – *The role that the verb 'to do' plays in negative sentences and questions*

The verb 'to do' is an irregular verb and an auxiliary verb, which means it can act like a modal by modifying the main verb in the sentence. It has different forms for its simple past tense and past participle.

Simple present: I/we/they **do**   he/she/it **does**

Simple past: I/we/they **did**   he/she/it **did**

Present perfect: I/we/they have **done**   he/she/it has **done**

The simple present forms need to be studied to avoid careless mistakes.

> *It is a simple strategy and **do not** solve the issue of poor attendance.* ✗
> *It is a simple strategy and **does not** solve the issue of poor attendance.* ✔

The verb is used to form 'yes/no' questions.

> *Do they have access to this information?*

But when forming questions, writers tend to mistakenly favour 'is' or 'are' and ignore the verb 'to do'.

> ***Are** female learners believe this as well?* ✗
> ***Do** female learners believe this as well?* ✔

> ***Is** the contribution of other countries change during these periods?* ✗
> ***Does** the contribution of other countries change during these periods?* ✔

Note how the main verb does not change from its normal or base form when the verb 'to do' is used, much like a modal.

*The level **increases** after a few successful runs.*

*Does the level **increase** after a few successful runs?*

*   *   *

Another issue relates to statements that contain interrogative terms. (See also 4.4.)

Question: How do they deal with this issue?

Statement with an interrogative term: We will look at how they deal with this issue.

This type of phrase is not a question and does not require the verb 'to do'.

*We will look at how **do they** try to change this issue.* ✘

*We will look at how **they** try to change this issue.* ✔

*All the respondents appear to have similar answers for how often **do they** like to participate.* ✘

*All the respondents appear to have similar answers for how often **they** like to participate.* ✔

> **!** 'Do' can also be used alongside modals. This next example does require 'do', but the modal 'should' is creating the error and has to change places with the subject.
>
> *It is also important to understand what should teachers do in this situation.* ✘
>
> *It is also important to understand what **teachers should do** in this situation.* ✔

Negative statements attract errors. When the negative form is required, writers tend to forget to include the verb (in this case 'do' not).

*However, studies about the oral gains in the SA environment **not** always receive positive results.* ✘

*However, studies about the oral gains in the SA environment **do not** always receive positive results.* ✔

*These resources **not** seem to be extensive enough for the number of students at the college.* ✘

*These resources **do not** seem to be extensive enough for the number of students at the college.* ✔

6.5 Exercises

A. Three sentences are correct and three incorrect. Can you identify them? Put an 'x' next to the ones that are wrong.

The next section would provide an evaluation of the three strategies. _____

We will also look at how they can improve their image? _____

Different teachers should sets different projects to ensure there is variety. _____

How does this affect their relationship with the staff? _____

It could be essential for all students to register their interest beforehand. _____

The reports does not include South America or Africa. _____

B. Select a suitable modal verb for each of these sentences (there is more than one possibility for some sentences).

can   could   will   would   should

The results _____ be available the following day if everything goes to plan.

_____ they reduce their spending while retaining the quality of their product?

Tan (2003) rejected the claim that they _____ enter both markets successfully.

This _____ be discussed in the following chapter.

I _____ have selected managers but decided that the opinions of ordinary workers _____ be more useful.

7

PREPOSITIONS AND PARTICLES

Focus on . . . Phrases containing prepositions

Phrasal verbs

This chapter provides lists of the most commonly confused phrases containing prepositions, with the main issue being wrong choice of preposition/particle. These mistakes can only be eliminated through exposure. The chapter also explores how phrasal verbs are formed and why they should be replaced with single verbs where possible.

Background / 7.1 choosing between 'on' and 'in' / 7.2 phrases that take 'to' / 7.3 other prepositional terms / 7.4 understanding phrasals / 7.5 Exercises

Featured errors in 7:

See lists (7.1, 7.2, 7.3, 7,4)	find out (7.4)	left out (7.4)
plus . . .	focus (7.1)	point (7.2)
access (7.2)	held up (7.4)	prior (7.2)
effect (7.1)	impact (7.1)	reach (7.2)
filled (7.4)	leading (7.2)	tried out (7.4)

BACKGROUND: Prepositions help to show the relationship between words in a sentence. Some have an obvious meaning when relating to the position of physical objects (under, above, on, in), but others like 'for' and 'of' are more difficult to define—they only really have meaning when they are used with other words.

Prepositions modify nouns and phrases and can explain how something happened, where something is, and what something is for.

*The device was put back **in** its sleeve and placed **on** the table **for** the next group.*

They are also used as time references.

*Employees were told that **from** the following week they would no longer be able to arrive **after** 9 a.m.*

Prepositions are followed by an object (a noun or pronoun) to form a prepositional phrase. These phrases can be short (*after 9 a.m.*) or quite long (*with a different outcome every time*).

See 15.2 for advice on which prepositions to use with dates, 15.4 for which prepositions to use for time periods, and 16.6 for which prepositions to use with numbers and amounts.

REVEALED: 7.1 – *Terms that create uncertainty over the use of 'on' and 'in'*

on average

*Participants buy these brands three times a year **in average**.* ✘
*Participants buy these brands three times a year **on average**.* ✔

based on

*This was **based in** his previous research about the industry.* ✘
*This was **based on** his previous research about the industry.* ✔

'Based in' can be used for location:

The company is based in Beijing.

on the basis (of)

*This was made **in the basis** of a stronger written constitution.* ✘

*This was made **on the basis** of a stronger written constitution.* ✔

concentrate on

*I will look to **concentrate in** the social issues of this trend.* ✘

*I will look to **concentrate on** the social issues of this trend.* ✔

in contrast

On contrast, the south is much poorer and lacking these resources. ✘

***In contrast**, the south is much poorer and lacking these resources.* ✔

dependent on/upon

*The prices have important implications for developing countries that are **dependent in** exports.* ✘

*The prices have important implications for developing countries that are **dependent on** exports.* ✔

invest in

Investing on internal R&D is a recent trend in the industry. ✘

***Investing in** internal R&D is a recent trend in the industry.* ✔

involved in

*The organization provides training opportunities for other stakeholders **involved on** running the business.* ✘

*The organization provides training opportunities for other stakeholders **involved in** running the business.* ✔

on . . . occasion

In a few occasions, the participants declined to answer. ✘

***On a few occasions**, the participants declined to answer.* ✔

participate in

*Twenty-four workers agreed to **participate on** the study.* ✘

*Twenty-four workers agreed to **participate in** the study.* ✔

on purpose

*It appears that the children are doing this **in purpose**.* ✘

*It appears that the children are doing this **on purpose**.* ✔

on the Internet/website

*This information has been made available **in the Internet/website**.* ✘

*This information has been made available **on the Internet/website**.* ✔

rely on

*The scheme does not simply **rely in** the countries having lower labour standards.* ✘

*The scheme does not simply **rely on** the countries having lower labour standards.* ✔

in this situation

***On this situation**, the introduction can create a more welcoming environment.* ✘

***In this situation**, the introduction can create a more welcoming environment.* ✔

in the long/short term

***On the long term**, these provisions should take effect.* ✘

***In the long term**, these provisions should take effect.* ✔

▶ RELATED ERRORS:

Using 'in' by mistake also occurs in the following phrases that all require 'on':

*This will have a considerable effect **in** society.* ✘

*This will have a considerable effect **on** society.* ✔

*It is important to focus **in** these failures.* ✘

*It is important to focus **on** these failures.* ✔

*They have a limited impact **in** intergovernmental relations in member states.* ✘

*They have a limited impact **on** intergovernmental relations in member states.* ✔

> ❗ This wrong selection of 'on' and 'in' is also apparent when choosing which of these prepositions to use for pages, sections, chapters, and tables. (See also 17.1.)
>
> *This can be located **in page 37**.* ✘
> *This can be located **on page 37**.* ✔
>
> ***On chapter four**, the weaknesses of both schemes are assessed.* ✘
> ***In chapter four**, the weaknesses of both schemes are assessed.* ✔
>
> *These will be discussed **on section three**.* ✘
> *These will be discussed **in section three**.* ✔
>
> *Some of these statistics are presented **on the table below**.* ✘
> *Some of these statistics are presented **in the table below**.* ✔
>
> Reports, studies, and papers all require 'in'.
>
> *Their roles are clarified **on** this new report.* ✘
> *Their roles are clarified **in** this new report.* ✔

REVEALED: 7.2 – *Terms that are followed by 'to'*

alternative to

*A possible **alternative with** relocating is to expand the site.* ✘
*A possible **alternative to** relocating is to expand the site.* ✔

applied to (to be suitable for)

*Also, they outline how the models can be **applied with** Japanese firms.* ✘
*Also, they outline how the models can be **applied to** Japanese firms.* ✔

assigned to

>*These participants will then be **assigned with** one of two groups.* ✘
>
>*These participants will then be **assigned to** one of two groups.* ✔

pay attention to

>*US companies pay more **attention on** long-term growth.* ✘
>
>*US companies pay more **attention to** long-term growth.* ✔

similar to

>*Their findings were **similar with** those obtained by Zavgren (1985).* ✘
>
>*Their findings were **similar to** those obtained by Zavgren (1985).* ✔

vulnerable to

>*It explains why these individuals might be **vulnerable from** changes in the environment.* ✘
>
>*It explains why these individuals might be **vulnerable to** changes in the environment.* ✔

▶ RELATED ERRORS:

Unsurprisingly given its size, 'to' can sometimes be overlooked. It needs to be included in the following terms:

>*... and hopefully **leading** relevant and effective outcomes.* ✘
>
>*... and hopefully **leading to** relevant and effective outcomes.* ✔

>***Prior** this there had been little support available.* ✘
>
>***Prior to** this there had been little support available.* ✔

>*This **points** a change in government policy on the issue.* ✘
>
>*This **points to** a change in government policy on the issue.* ✔

In these cases 'to' is not required.

>*They should be able to **access to** the database from any device.* ✘
>
>*They should be able to **access** the database from any device.* ✔

The noun does take 'to'.

There was no access to the system.

*The adult can **reach to** 15 cm when fully grown.* ✘

*The adult can **reach** 15 cm when fully grown.* ✔

REVEALED: 7.3 – *Other terms that attract the wrong prepositions*

accompanied by

*This is usually **accompanied with** a reduction in exports.* ✘

*This is usually **accompanied by** a reduction in exports.* ✔

associated with

*It is **associated to** a lack of support and encouragement.* ✘

*It is **associated with** a lack of support and encouragement.* ✔

benefit from

*They might also **benefit with** the greater investment in training.* ✘

*They might also **benefit from** the greater investment in training.* ✔

caused by

*This was likely to have been **caused with** a weak connection.* ✘

*This was likely to have been **caused by** a weak connection.* ✔

combine with

*It is possible to **combine** this **to** counselling sessions.* ✘

*It is possible to **combine** this **with** counselling sessions.* ✔

composed of

*The index is primarily **composed by** the prices of traditional exports.* ✘

*The index is primarily **composed of** the prices of traditional exports.* ✔

'Composed by' can be used for referring to someone who created something.

*The soundtrack was **composed by** Chen Yi.*

in conjunction with

The angle in conjunction to these joint parameters affects the dynamics during the task. ✘

*The angle **in conjunction with** these joint parameters affects the dynamics during the task.* ✔

consist of

The system consists with three parts, which will be discussed in turn. ✘

*The system **consists of** three parts, which will be discussed in turn.* ✔

But when writing 'consistent' use 'with'.

This is consistent to previous research.

*This is consistent **with** previous research.*

except for

All social enterprises in the sample, except of E5, have relied on grants to start their activities. ✘

*All social enterprises in the sample, **except for** E5, have relied on grants to start their activities.* ✔   (See also 12.1.)

likelihood of

It shows the likelihood for an event taking place in the next few months. ✘

*It shows the **likelihood of** an event taking place in the next few months.* ✔

need for

These results highlight the need of studies on this issue. ✘

*These results highlight the **need for** studies on this issue.* ✔

But 'need of' can be used with 'in' and as a plural.

be in need of—to need attention, help, money, etc.

*The company is **in need of** a modern IT system.*

needs (n)—what someone requires in order to live a normal healthy life

*They must address the **needs of** these marginal groups.*

reason for

*One **reason of** this is the difficulty in training all the staff.* ✘

*One **reason for** this is the difficulty in training all the staff.* ✔

responsible for

*This crisis is **responsible in** the poor results in these quarters.* ✘

*This crisis is **responsible for** the poor results in these quarters.* ✔

Also, you can be 'responsible to' a person or group of people.

*These employees are **responsible to** their respective line managers.*

result in

*The component method will **result to** a more accurate forecast.* ✘

*The component method will **result in** a more accurate forecast.* ✔

'Result from' means to be caused by.

*The bad grade **resulted from** a lack of critical analysis.*

verified by

*This will be developed and **verified with** the research team and relevant experts.* ✘

*This will be developed and **verified by** the research team and relevant experts.* ✔

REVEALED: 7.4 – *What phrasal verbs are and which particles to select*

Phrasal verbs are multipart verbs that comprise a verb and a preposition or an adverb (called a particle in a phrasal verb). They are different from other phrases that contain prepositions in that the meaning of the whole is not obvious if the parts of the phrasal verb are considered separately.

They must look after this equipment for several weeks.

(The individual meanings of the terms 'look' and 'after' do not help to explain the phrase.)

These verbs tend to end in directional words such as 'on', 'down', 'out', and 'back', but they are being used in an abstract way and judging them can be difficult. Many phrasal verbs are considered colloquial or examples of informal language, so single-word verbs are preferable (e.g., 'begin' is preferred to 'start off'); but some have an important part to play in academic descriptive writing and can certainly be useful once their meaning has been grasped and their use understood. A few phrasal verbs appeared earlier in the chapter, and some others are listed here:

act on/upon	add on	back down	break away
break up	bring about	cover up	cut out
depend on	help out	look into	look after
phase out	rule out	scale down	set up
shut down	team up	tell apart	type in

As mentioned, the single-word verb is normally a better option than a phrasal if available.

Unfortunately, this further held up the procedure. ✘
*Unfortunately, this further **delayed** the procedure.* ✔

Most of these responses were left out of the analysis. ✘
*Most of these responses were **omitted** from the analysis.* ✔

They tried out the software beforehand to ensure it ran smoothly. ✘
*They **tested** the software beforehand to ensure it ran smoothly.* ✔

▷ RELATED ERRORS:

Questionnaires and forms can be 'filled out' or 'filled in' but not just 'filled'. The example below needs to be rewritten to include one of the prepositions.

*These questionnaires were **filled by** the parents or guardian.* ✗

*   *   *

There is a subtle difference between 'to find' and 'to find out'. When reporting on the experience of a researcher and what the experience revealed, use 'find' instead of the phrasal verb.

*Leung (2009) **finds out** that children will respond well to this type of support.* ✗

*Leung (2009) **finds** that children will respond well to this type of support.* ✔

7.5 Exercises

A. Fill in the gaps with the correct particle/preposition.

A discussion of these theories will take place _____ chapter seven.

Prior _____ becoming CEO, she worked in the public sector.

Only pupils that had a good disciplinary record could participate _____ the scheme.

Each participant was then assigned _____ one of five groups.

This could result _____ confusion, as the two departments would be dealing with the same cases.

Hopefully, this will address the needs _____ the marginalized groups.

In most cases this leads _____ prosecution, so it is more than worthwhile.

B. Match the particle to the root word. One has already been done.

result   by

caused   from

rely   on

likelihood   in

benefit   with

combine   of

8
ADJECTIVES AND ADVERBS

Focus on . . . Adjectives

Adverbs and conjunctive adverbs

Other sentence starters

This chapter covers adjectives and adverbs and explores how both are used in English. It addresses adjectives that compare things and how some terms must employ different means to form a comparison. Conjunctive adverbs are introduced and assessed along with some commonly misused sentence starters and phrases.

Background / 8.1 adjective and adverb *–ly* / 8.2 adverb position /
8.3 difference between the participles / 8.4 comparative adjectives /
8.5 'in'+adjective or adverb / 8.6 conjunctive adverbs /
8.7 other sentence starters / 8.8 Exercises

Featured errors in 8:

additional (8.6)	less (8.2)	positive (8.1)
as (8.7)	lowest (8.4)	predominantly (8.2)
compared with (8.4)	meanwhile (8.7)	previous (8.6)
economically (8.5)	more (8.2)	realistic (8.6)
high / highly (8.1)	most (8.4)	recently (8.5)
however (8.6)	negative (8.1)	regarding (8.7)
in other words (8.7)	on the other hand (8.7)	specific (8.5)
in particular (8.5)	overall (8.5)	than (8.4)
in the meantime (8.7)	particularly (8.5)	tiring (8.3)
least (8.4)	politically (8.5)	with (8.7)

BACKGROUND: Adjectives are versatile in that they can describe, identify, and quantify. They are used to modify nouns and pronouns.

The noun 'country' can be modified by an adjective in the following ways:

Describe: *An underdeveloped country*   Identify: *The next country*

Quantify: *Three countries*

As seen above, the adjective usually goes before the noun. But when adjectives are describing size or shape they can appear after the noun.

   *The poster was ten metres **long** and six metres **wide**.*

(See 14.3 and 16.2 for advice on the order of adjectives in a sentence.)

Adverbs are similar to adjectives, but they modify verbs instead of nouns. Many, but not all, adverbs end in –*ly*.

   *The industry has changed **rapidly** in the past few years.*

Adverbs can be split into categories based on how they modify.

Manner: recently, quickly, loudly

   They attended a conference recently.

Place: nearby, outside, everywhere

   There is another research centre nearby.

Time: after, before, soon

   A focus group will also meet soon.

Adverbs also modify adjectives and other adverbs.

Frequency: never, often, always

   It is often difficult to extract information using this method.

Degree: quite, extremely, very

   The patients revealed that they found this process quite stressful.

REVEALED: 8.1 – *The mistakes that are made when choosing between an adjective and its adverb form (–ly)*

Not all adverbs end in *–ly* but a common error that writers make is using the adjective form instead of the *–ly* adverb when a verb or another adjective is being modified.

> *Understandably, job engagement is **positive related** to job satisfaction.* ✗
>
> *Understandably, job engagement is **positively related** to job satisfaction.* ✔
>
> *As a result, it is usually **perceived negative** and not favoured by senior management.* ✗
>
> *As a result, it is usually **perceived negatively** and not favoured by senior management.* ✔

Here are further examples. First, an adjective (*high*) is used with another adjective when it should be an adverb (*highly*) doing the modifying. Second, an adverb (*highly*) is modifying a noun (*turnout*) when it should be an adjective (*high*).

> *In the next section we will be focusing on **high skilled** employees.* ✗
>
> *In the next section we will be focusing on **highly skilled** employees.* ✔
>
> *In the 2000 election there was a **highly** turnout.* ✗
>
> *In the 2000 election there was a **high** turnout.* ✔

> Compounds that contain an adverb ending in *–ly* should not have a hyphen. The following mistake is a common one made by writers:
>
> *The exhibits included a richly-decorated vase.* ✗
> *The exhibits included a richly decorated vase.* ✔

REVEALED: 8.2 – *Where to place an adverb in a sentence*

Adverbs are most effective when appearing before the word that they are modifying. And when the word being modified is an adjective, the adverb must come before it.

*This was **significantly changed** when the new government took over.*

But adverbs that describe how something is done, adverbs of time, and adverbial phrases can be found after the modified word and at the end of a sentence.

*This output **decreases slowly** until the final quarter.*

*The drone was then able to fly **over the campus**.*

The adverb comes after forms of the verb 'to be'.

*The system **frequently is** checked for errors.* ✗

*The system **is frequently** checked for errors.* ✔

* * *

A subtle mistake, but one that will be noticed by readers whose first language is English, is placing the adverb before the verb instead of next to the adverbial phrase it should be modifying. The following example demonstrates this:

*The issue **predominantly** occurs in the poorer regions of the country.* ✗

*The issue occurs **predominantly** in the poorer regions of the country.* ✔

The adverb 'predominantly' should be modifying the phrase 'in the poorer regions . . .' and not the verb 'occurs'.

▷ RELATED ERRORS:

'More' and 'less' can be used as adjectives (first example) and adverbs (second and third examples below). Note the correct position in these sets of sentences.

*There should be **focus more** on supporting these minorities.* ✗

*There should be **more focus** on supporting these minorities.* ✔

*They should **more focus** on supporting these minorities.* ✗

*They should **focus more** on supporting these minorities.* ✔

*They **less agreed** about whether the system should be available to non-members.* ✗

*They **agreed less** about whether the system should be available to non-members.* ✔

REVEALED: 8.3 – *How to differentiate between a present participle and a past participle*

The present and past participles can be used like adjectives, as seen in 5.3–5.6. There is an important rule to help recognize when a present participle or a past participle should be used. If the person or thing is the cause of the effect, then the present participle (*–ing*) is needed.

> *The presentation was **embarrassing**, as the students had not prepared properly and had little to say.*

If the person or thing is experiencing the effect, then the past participle (usually '–ed') is used.

> *The student felt **embarrassed** by the grade and sought advice from the tutor.*

By using the information above, this common error below can be understood and corrected.

> *Some of the participants might feel **tiring** after four consecutive tasks.* ✗
> *Some of the participants might feel **tired** after four consecutive tasks.* ✔

Note below how an outcome is being described in the first example, and a person's feelings about the outcome are being reported in the second.

> *This is **disappointing** given the resources that were available.*
> *They were **disappointed** with the outcome of the study.*

REVEALED: 8.4 – *How to use comparative adjectives*

Adjectives can be used to compare things with three degrees of comparison possible (e.g., high, higher, highest). 'Than' is used to complete the comparative (middle) form as seen below.

> *Poverty levels of the minority group living in urban China were also **higher than** that of the majority group.*

Adjectives in the first degree (e.g., high) do not technically compare so cannot be used with 'than'. In other words, if there is not a comparing word in the sentence, 'than' should not be used. 'Compared with' can be used to form a comparison instead.

*This rate is low **than** the results from the second sample.* ✘

*This rate is low **compared with** the results from the second sample.* ✔

When there is an apparent choice between the two terms, opt for 'than' if the adjective is in the comparative degree and the two things are being evaluated directly.

*The levels were also much greater **compared with** the companies in group two.* ✘

*The levels were also much greater **than** those of the companies in group two.* ✔

> Sometimes 'than' is omitted by mistake.
>
> *The exports were **higher** the imports during this period.* ✘
> *The exports were higher **than** the imports during this period.* ✔
>
> (See also 12.1.)

Two superlatives known to be a source of confusion are 'least' and 'lowest'. 'Lowest' is the superlative form of low (low, lower, lowest). 'Least' is technically the superlative form of 'little' but is mainly used for modifying other adjectives and adverbs to mean the smallest extent or less than anything else.

*This is the **lowest** abundant species in the region.* ✘

*This is the **least** abundant species in the region.* ✔

'Least' is used with uncountable nouns and describes amount.

*The country also has the **least** number of female engineers.* ✘

*The country also has the **lowest** number of female engineers.* ✔

*   *   *

Some adjectives cannot form these different degrees of comparison by changing their endings like 'low' can, so they use 'more'/'less' and 'most'/'least' instead. A common error is failing to recognize the ones that can.

*This logo showed the **most close** association with trustworthiness and reliability.* ✘

*This logo showed the **closest** association with trustworthiness and reliability.* ✔

REVEALED: 8.5 – *Errors associated with the use of 'in' before adverbs and adjectives*

The adjective 'particular' can be preceded by 'in' to form the following phrase:

*They were interested in the use of these genes **in particular**.*

'In' cannot be used with the adverb form.

*This is **in particularly** useful for comparing strategies across disciplines.* ✘
*This is **particularly** useful for comparing strategies across disciplines.* ✔

The adverb 'particularly' is used either before a verb or to begin a sentence as an adverbial (see 8.6), whereas the phrase 'in particular' is often found at the end of the sentence.

Mistakes also occur with 'specific', 'overall', and 'recently'.

***In specific**, these regions were created as a 'test base' for liberalization.* ✘
***Specifically**, these regions were created as a 'test base' for liberalization.* ✔

***In overall**, the improvement has been minimal.* ✘
***Overall**, the improvement has been minimal.* ✔

***In recently**, this growth has slowed . . .* ✘
***Recently**, this growth has slowed . . .* ✔

▶ RELATED ERRORS:

The tendency to use in + adjective instead of the correct adverb form can also be seen after the verb, as in these examples.

*The policy has failed both **in political** and **in economic**.* ✘
*The policy has failed both **politically** and **economically**.* ✔

*This item is also produced **in local**.* ✘
*This item is also produced **locally**.* ✔

REVEALED: 8.6 – *The use and misuse of conjunctive adverbs*

Conjunctive adverbs (furthermore, however, meanwhile . . .) should be used sparingly. Often there is no need to begin the clause with one.

> *This study examines efficiency measures using the new model;* **however***, many studies have examined efficiency including Morgan and Jones (2009) . . .* ✘

> *This study examines efficiency measures using the new model. Many studies have examined efficiency, including Morgan and Jones (2009) . . .* ✔

It is important to study their meanings, because some are appropriate only in certain situations.

'However' is often misused by writers. It does not mean 'next' or 'additionally'.

> *Table 2 indicates the overall average mean and the standard deviation among 200 respondents.* **However***, the mean for engagement is 3.54 and the standard deviation is 0.50.* ✘

'However' means 'on the other hand' or 'yet/nevertheless' and is used to introduce a statement that contrasts with the previous one.

> *The contribution from salary increased from 22% to 30% in this period;* **however***, the contribution from the government declined during this time.*

'However' is also used to begin a clause, rather than a new sentence, as it implies the continuation of a point. (See 10 and 19.3.)

▷ **RELATED ERRORS:**

Some adverbs can begin sentences as adverbials. They modify the whole of the sentence that follows. Many of them end in *–ly* but the suffix is often omitted by writers, leaving an incorrect adjective form.

> *Additional, a quarter of the country's students leave university or technical college without graduating.* ✘

> **Additionally***, a quarter of the country's students leave university or technical college without graduating.* ✔

> *Realistic, we need to assume that the response rate will be no higher than 75% given the sensitive nature of the questions.* ✘

Realistically, *we need to assume that the response rate will be no higher than 75% given the sensitive nature of the questions.* ✔

Previous, *they had attempted to do this without a set schedule.* ✗

Previously, *they had attempted to do this without a set schedule.* ✔

REVEALED: 8.7 *– The mistakes made when using other sentence or clause starters*

Writers often use 'as' instead of 'with' to mean accompanying.

As *the emergence of globalization, CSR has become an important element that a large enterprise cannot ignore.* ✗

With *the emergence of globalization, CSR has become an important element that a large enterprise cannot ignore.* ✔

At the beginning of a sentence 'with' can mean 'accompanying' or 'in relation to'.

With *the new position comes much more responsibility.*

With *previous projects they found that the best solution was to bring in consultants.*

At the beginning of a sentence 'as' can mean 'because' or 'given that'.

As *the market had deteriorated, the company decided to withdraw.*

As *the teacher spoke, the students finally began to settle down.*

At the start of a sentence 'as' begins a dependent clause, meaning a second part of the sentence is required. Writers often add an 'as' unnecessarily when there is no additional part.

As *Li (2010) proposed that a new framework should be applied to motivation studies.* ✗

Li (2010) proposed that a new framework should be applied to motivation studies. ✔

Or perhaps the writer meant to write,

As *Li (2010) proposed, a new framework should be applied to motivation studies.* ✔

'As' and 'with' can be used together to mean 'as we find in' or 'as is true of'.

> **As with** *any campaign, the level of funding proved crucial.*

*   *   *

A few more phrases that act as sentence starters and that produce errors are listed next.

There is no such phrase as 'regarding to'. The 'to' should not be included; the mistake may stem from the similarity to 'according to'.

> **Regarding to** *nationalities, the author only interviewed American companies in Japan.* ✘
>
> **Regarding** *nationalities, the author only interviewed American companies in Japan.* ✔

Regarding means 'with regard to' or 'concerning'. Another common mistake is to write 'in regard with'. Use one of the following instead:

regarding, in regard to, with regard to, as regards

> **In regard with** *the financial problems facing the company . . .* ✘
>
> **With regard to/Regarding** *the financial problems facing the company . . .* ✔

*   *   *

A phrase that is overused and misused is 'in the meantime'.

> **In the meantime**, *testing was carried out on SMEs in the local area.*

Writers often put the following:

> **In the meanwhile**, *I was busy researching the second topic.* ✘

But 'meanwhile' stands on its own and has no prepositions associated with it.

> **Meanwhile**, *I was busy researching the second topic.* ✔

Note also that 'meantime' is one word.

> *In the* **mean time**, *the plan is to initiate a formal discussion with the participants to gauge their general views on the topic.* ✘

*   *   *

Another misused phrase is 'on the other hand'. It does not have the same meaning as 'also' so cannot be used as an additional thought. It is used for giving a contrasting viewpoint or applying caution to what has been said before.

> *I will address these issues in section four.* **On the other hand** *this section also covers political reasons for the failure . . .* ✘

> *I will address these issues in section four. This section also covers political reasons for the failure . . .* ✔

Here is an example of the phrase being used accurately.

> **On one hand**, *the taskforce has taken steps to ensure this does not end up being a significant issue in the region.* **On the other hand**, *its mere presence does indicate a potential problem in the long term.*

Unsurprisingly, a common mistake is to write 'in' instead of 'on'.

> *In one hand . . . in the other hand*

> **On one hand . . . on the other hand**

*   *   *

The following variations of this next phrase are all incorrect:

> *in another word*   *in different words*   *With other words*

The correct form is 'in other words'.

> *In another word*, *they are responsible for planning and setting the rules and regulations.* ✘

> **In other words**, *they are responsible for planning and setting the rules and regulations.* ✔

(See 2.5 for more fixed phrases.)

8.8 Exercises

A. In the following sentences, select the correct comparative form.

As Table 5 shows, the [most high / higher / highest] amount was recorded in Q2.

Less than 2% lost their jobs [more than / than / compared with] 4% the year before.

These figures were [low / lower / lowest] than expected, considering many of their competitors had improved their positions.

These findings reveal 'InterTrain' to be the [most strong / stronger / strongest] brand of the five companies.

It has proven to be the [less / least / lowest] effective with the [least / lowest / low] scores across all four tests.

B. Change the incorrect adverbs (–_ly_) into adjectives in this extract and vice versa.

Given the current globally competitiveness in this industry, if companies can find a way to conduct business effectively it will give them a clearly advantage over their rivals. Similar, if negotiations can be carried out efficiently and promptly, then more time can be devoted to research and development (R&D)—the focus of this paper. A high regarded study on R&D is Sheridan and Lo (2013), who looked at the frequently failure of three firms attempting to enhance their R&D output.

9
POSSESSION AND COMPOUNDS

Focus on . . . Possession

Compounds

The 'of' phrase

This chapter looks at how to express possession correctly in a sentence and the instances where possession does not occur. The chapter presents the different structures related to possession, including the 'of' phrase and generic compound. It also clarifies the placement of the plural term in certain phrases.

Background / 9.1 the possessive apostrophe / 9.2 compound phrases / 9.3 'of' phrases and which to select / 9.4 Exercises

Featured errors in 9:

conflict of interest (9.3)	level of intensity (9.3)
earning (9.2)	point of view (9.3)
et al. (9.3)	school of thought (9.3)
its (9.1)	

BACKGROUND: The apostrophe is used to indicate both possession and contraction. For possession, it shows that something belongs to someone or something, or to a group. Note that the apostrophe comes before the 's' for these singular nouns and after the 's' for the plural nouns.

Noun	Singular possessive	Plural possessive
author	author's	authors'
country	country's	countries'
participant	participant's	participants'

The **authors'** biographies are presented at the end of the paper. (plural: more than one author)

The **author's** biography is presented at the end of the paper. (singular: one author)

(See 3B for possessive pronoun use.)

REVEALED: 9.1 – When to use the possessive apostrophe

There seems to be an urge to use the possessive apostrophe with almost every plural noun. In the example below, there is no possession, so no apostrophe is required.

The **participants'** were then asked to remove their blindfolds and carry out the task normally. ✗

The **participants** were then asked to remove their blindfolds and carry out the task normally. ✔

▶ RELATED ERRORS:

Of course, the classic possessive error is its/it's.

its: The most important feature is **it's** flexibility. ✗

The most important feature is **its** flexibility. ✔

it's = (it is): They also pointed out that **it's** a lot cheaper than the other schemes.

Note that contractions should be avoided in academic writing. (See also 13.1.)

REVEALED: 9.2 – *How compounds are formed and when they should be chosen over possessive phrases*

Some terms involve two or more nouns (or adjectives and nouns) in a row to form a single phrase that is considered a single unit. Most of these compounds have a generic, uncountable meaning rather than detailing an actual situation. The initial word acts like an adjective (even though it may be a noun) and modifies the other word(s). But when the first word is a noun as in these next examples, the temptation is to use the plural form or possession.

*They used genetic switches for **biomarkers detection**.* ✗
*They used genetic switches for **biomarker detection**.* ✔

***Students' learning** has been measured by three different scales.* ✗
***Student learning** has been measured by three different scales.* ✔

*In this way, **researchers bias** can be reduced.* ✗
*In this way, **researcher bias** can be reduced.* ✔

Possession is not suitable because these compound phrases are generic and not describing specific instances. And this next example is not referring to a particular person but to adults in general and therefore the adult population in general.

*Most studies have analysed the local **adult's** population.* ✗
*Most studies have analysed the local **adult** population.* ✔

The pluralized error also appears when units of time are used in a standard adjective phrase. (See also 15.5.)

*The participants had less than a **ten minutes walk** to the meeting room.* ✗
*The participants had less than a **ten-minute walk** to the meeting room.* ✔

*There was a **two hours** break between these lectures.* ✗
*There was a **two-hour** break between these lectures.* ✔

There are a few terms that are exceptions to this singular modifier rule.

systems *analyst*   ***admissions*** *policy*   ***earnings*** *forecast*

The words in bold are commonly used in the plural form in their respective fields even when modifying.

*This subfield is known as **earning** management.* ✘

*This subfield is known as **earnings** management.* ✔

REVEALED: 9.3 *– The relationships among 'of' phrases, possessive phrases, and compounds*

There are usually three options available to the writer when forming these types of phrases. They are evaluated here using the words 'system' and 'design'.

Some tutors of English believe that the possessive should not be used for inanimate objects and an 'of phrase' should be employed instead.

*The **design of the system** was prioritized by the team.*

Others see no reason why the possessive form should not be used.

*The **system's design** was prioritized by the team.*

But these options are only available if a particular system is being referred to. Otherwise, the sentence is generic and the compound is required.

***System design** is an important part of this process.*

The following error is common:

System's design was prioritized by the team. ✘

This is neither possession nor a compound and is therefore not an option. If it was meant to be a specific system and possessive, then it would require an article as in the second example above.

If it was meant to be a generic reference, then it would be written without an apostrophe and without an article.

> **System design** *was prioritized by the team.* ✔

*   *   *

Some terms are written as 'of' phrases instead of combining to form compounds. When these phrases are plural, the first word is plural but the second part remains singular.

> *We were hoping to extract different* **point of views** *from the employees in the focus group.* ✘

> *We were hoping to extract different* **points of view** *from the employees in the focus group.* ✔

The following are also common errors related to this construction:

conflict of interests	**conflicts** of interest
level of intensities	**levels** of intensity
school of thoughts	**schools** of thought

Equally, 'of' phrases can be overused and are even inappropriate in some situations. The following are two extreme examples:

> **The performance of it** *is also assessed from the perspectives of the end user.* ✘

> **Its performance** *is also assessed from the perspectives of the end user.* ✔

> *In the section of methodology the key terms were defined.* ✘

> **In the methodology (section)** *the key terms were defined.* ✔

▷ **RELATED ERRORS:**

The 'of' phrase is probably the best choice when showing possession for more than two authors (i.e., when the reference contains et al.). Using the apostrophe (et al.'s) has an awkward appearance.

> *Williams et al. (1999)'s suggestion is an interesting one.* ✘

> *Williams et al. (1999's) suggestion is an interesting one.* ✘

> **The suggestion of Williams et al. (1999)** *is an interesting one.* ✔

9.4 Exercises

A. Select the correct term from the options below and complete the sentences.

country   country's   countrys'   countries   countries'

This could prove difficult for _____ not signing up to this scheme.

I will focus on five Asian _____ for answering question five.

I will also look at this _____ attitude towards consumer rights.

Most _____ policies differ in this respect, so it will require a deep analysis.

B. Fill in the gaps by picking the most appropriate phrase from the options.

native population   native's population   natives population
natives' population

A distinction should be made between this cohort and the _____.

four hour   four hour's   four hours   four hours'

The session was _____ long and covered the key topics.

three-steps   three's-step   three-step   three-step's

A _____ framework is now proposed that seeks to resolve this issue.

manager viewpoints   manager viewpoint   manager's viewpoint
managers' viewpoint

This particular _____ is captured through a questionnaire and an interview.

10
CLAUSES AND OTHER STRUCTURES

Focus on ... Clauses

Irregular sentence structure

Lists

Negative statements

The chapter begins by presenting the two main types of clause and how they function in a sentence. It then introduces certain phrases that can begin and link clauses, including the troublesome term 'that'. The chapter explains a few irregular sentence constructions before finishing with some guidance on forming lists and negative sentences.

Background / 10.1 'which', 'where', and 'whereas' /
10.2 connecting clauses and 'although' / 10.3 leaving out 'that' /
10.4 'not only ... but also' / 10.5 comparative construction /
10.6 writing lists / 10.7 forming negative sentences / 10.8 Exercises

Featured errors in 10:

also (10.4)	firstly (10.6)	such as (10.6)
although (10.2)	no (10.7)	that (10.3)
at last (10.6)	not (10.7)	where (10.1)
but (10.2, 10.4)	not only (10.4)	which (10B, 10.1)
etc. (10.6)	only with/if (10.4)	
even though (10.2)	rather (10.4)	

BACKGROUND: Every sentence has a main clause that contains a subject and a verb. Main clauses are also known as independent clauses because they can stand on their own without requiring any additional information. They represent a complete idea or thought.

The government is currently tackling this issue.

A dependent clause 'depends' on the independent (main) clause for its meaning, so it cannot be used on its own. It is only part of a sentence and not a complete thought.

Which will be a difficult task.

This is an incomplete thought, and there must be some information before it.

*The speaker must keep this audience interested for two hours, **which will be a difficult task**.*

If the clause beginning with 'which' is left out, the sentence will still make sense because the first clause is an independent one.

REVEALED: 10.1 – *When to choose 'which', 'where', and 'whereas'*

'Which' is inserted unnecessarily into main (independent) clauses by writers. It is primarily used to begin dependent ones.

*These stocks **which** are picked from the FTSE 100.* ✗
These stocks are picked from the FTSE 100. ✔

Here is a typical way to employ 'which'.

*The stocks are picked from the FTSE 100, **which** is a share index on the London Stock Exchange.*

'That' can be used to begin a phrase modifying the first part of an independent clause.

*They looked at the cases **which** had occurred in the last two months.* ✗
*They looked at the cases **that** had occurred in the last two months.* ✔

'Which' is also mistakenly used instead of 'where'/'in which' for expressing location or place.

> First we analyse China, **which** Zhang and Xu (2014) have conducted some interesting research. ✘
>
> First we analyse China, **where** Zhang and Xu (2014) have conducted some interesting research. ✔

But 'where' should be replaced with 'whereas' when there is contrast or a comparison.

> Tan (1998) focused on the lack of funding and support from the government, **where** Lin (2007) listed the welfare schemes the government had implemented. ✘
>
> Tan (1998) focused on the lack of funding and support from the government, **whereas** Lin (2007) listed the welfare schemes the government had implemented. ✔

▷ RELATED ERRORS:

The verb 'to be' is often missed out in error when 'which' is used.

> This is dependent on acquiring the latest technology, which a further cost that the organization has to manage. ✘
>
> This is dependent on acquiring the latest technology, **which is** a further cost that the organization has to manage. ✔
>
> These issues, which a permanent source of confusion, can only be addressed by … ✘
>
> These issues, **which are** a permanent source of confusion, can only be addressed by … ✔

REVEALED: 10.2 – *When to connect clauses and how to use 'although'*

Connecting clauses can be a real problem for some writers. This first example consists of one clause when two are actually required. A main verb ('was' in this case) has been used at the start, but this leads to confusion when the reader meets another main verb ('indicated') a little further along.

*Another influential study by Kim (2001) **was about how their expectancies might influence the potential performance of students** indicated that these effects can occur outside the classroom.*

This first part would be fine as a standalone sentence.

Another influential study by Kim (2001) was about how their expectancies might influence the potential performance of students.

A better construction for the entire sentence could be achieved by removing the first verb and putting a dependent clause between two commas.

*Another influential study by Kim (2001), **about how their expectancies might influence the potential performance of students**, indicated that these effects can occur outside the classroom.* ✔

(See also 19.1 and 19.3 for punctuation use in clauses.)

*   *   *

'Although' is used at the beginning of dependent clauses. If a comma is used directly after 'although', it is difficult to follow the meaning of the sentence.

***Although**, there was considerable variation in the range of values among individuals, all of them displayed symptoms.* ✘

***Although** there was considerable variation . . .* ✔

'Although' can be used AFTER a comma to begin an additional thought, and in a moderating phrase BETWEEN commas.

*The target to aim for is N5, **although** the method works equally well for other standards.*

*The literature on multivariate analysis, **although** extensive, is widely scattered.*

▷ RELATED ERRORS:

A sentence beginning with 'even though' will also need an additional clause for it to make sense.

Even though Chomsky did not examine this. ✘

*Even though Chomsky did not examine this, **he did distinguish between 'strict rules' and 'selectional rules'**.* ✔

The connecting term 'but' should not begin the main clause. This is a common mistake when the dependent clause starts with 'even though' or 'although'.

> Even though the sample was large, **but** the results proved inconclusive. ✘
>
> Even though the sample was large, the results proved inconclusive. ✔

REVEALED: 10.3 – *When to leave out 'that' in a sentence*

It is sometimes difficult to know when to leave out 'that' and when to retain it.

When 'that' begins a dependent clause that is the OBJECT of the sentence, it can usually be omitted. Normally there is a personal pronoun present ('they' below).

> The amount of time (**that**) they take is also considered.

When 'that' is part of a phrase modifying the SUBJECT ('SMEs' below), then it should not be omitted.

> The SMEs were previously rejected will also be included in this sample. ✘
>
> The SMEs **that** were previously rejected will also be included in this sample. ✔

Here is another example where 'that' is crucial to the sentence:

> Market efficiency and accounting qualities are two major factors influence this. ✘
>
> Market efficiency and accounting qualities are two major factors **that** influence this. ✔

> The other option for the writer is the *–ing* form.
>
> *Market efficiency and accounting qualities are two major factors influencing this.*

Here, 'that' is required to modify the phrase in the first part of the sentence.

> There are few studies have looked at the long-term effects . . . ✘
>
> There are few studies **that** have looked at the long-term effects . . . ✔

But the first part is not really necessary (There are), and this means neither is 'that'.

*Few studies **that** have looked at the long-term effects . . .* ✘

Few studies have looked at the long-term effects . . . ✔

If in doubt, read the sentence with and without 'that'. This may help to determine whether it can be omitted or not.

▷ **RELATED ERRORS:**

Writers needlessly insert 'that' into a whole host of sentences.

*The reason is because **that** there is no internal support from the institution.* ✘

The reason is because there is no internal support from the institution. ✔

*This is a new development, so **that** they are eager to understand its impact.* ✘

This is a new development, so they are eager to understand its impact. ✔

*It did not arise in other firms **that** with lower liquidation.* ✘

It did not arise in other firms with lower liquidation. ✔

This next example is a typical error. There is a choice here between 'that is' or omitting the phrase, but the writer chooses the option that is not available—'that'.

*Rong (2011) states that this would only occur in an industry **that** lacking information.* ✘

Rong (2011) states that this would only occur in an industry that is lacking information. ✔

Rong (2011) states that this would only occur in an industry lacking information. ✔

REVEALED: 10.4 – *How to form the phrase 'not only . . . but also'*

Some sentence constructions go against the normal rules and show inversion despite being statements and not questions; for instance, the subject and verb are reversed when using the adverbial clause 'not only' at the start of the sentence. Writers understandably place the subject before the verb.

*Not only **the number is** wrong but also the placement.* ✘

*Not only **is the number** wrong but also the placement.* ✔

The verb 'to do' should not be added to the phrase.

> They **did not only change** the number of firms but also the industry in which they conducted their business. ✘

> They **not only changed** the number of firms but also the industry in which they conducted their business. ✔

When a modal is included, the first part is again inverted. And the position of 'also' should be noted.

> **Not only they must** have knowledge of the different strategies, but also they must have enough influence to impose them. ✘

> **Not only must they** have knowledge of the different strategies, but **they must also** have enough influence to impose them. ✔

> Avoid the form 'not only . . . but rather', as this does not make sense.
>
> In this first example the writer wished to show difference, not connection.
>
> They **not only** utilized the usual plastic **but rather** liquid wood. ✘
>
> They **did not** utilize the usual plastic **but rather** liquid wood. ✔
>
> Here the writer DID want to give an additional example, so
>
> 'not only . . . but also' can be used.
>
> They **not only** used published letters **but rather** personal correspondence. ✘
>
> They not only used published letters **but also** personal correspondence. ✔

A similar phrase begins 'only with/if . . .'. This time the second part is inverted.

> Only with the support of the board members **can the scheme be implemented**.

The second part on its own would form a question normally.

> Can the scheme be implemented? (See also 4.4 and 6.4.)

REVEALED: 10.5 – *How to form the comparative phrase*

Another irregular sentence construction is the comparative one.

The higher the price, the lower the satisfaction rating.

Both parts begin with 'the', and the verb 'to be' is often omitted. Writers usually make one of the following four errors:

*The higher **is** the price, the **lower satisfaction** rating.* ✗

*The higher the price **is**, the lower **is** the satisfaction rating.* ✗

*The higher the price, **lower** the satisfaction rating.* ✗

*The **higher price**, the **lower satisfaction** rating.* ✗

REVEALED: 10.6 – *Key errors when writing lists*

When creating lists, there are a few rules to follow.

When stating all the options and how many there are, the phrases 'such as' and 'including' are not necessary.

*This is split into four categories **such as**, fully trained, newly trained, partly trained, and untrained.* ✗

This is split into four categories: fully trained, newly trained, partly trained, and untrained. ✔

'First, second, third . . .' are preferred to 'firstly, secondly, thirdly . . .'

***Firstly**, the three schemes will be examined; **secondly** . . .* ✗

***First**, the three schemes will be examined; **second** . . .* ✔

(See also 16.4.)

* * *

The phrase 'at last' should never end a list. It sounds as though the writer is relieved it is over.

*. . . third, I will address the main concerns of the four stakeholders; **at last**, I will offer a conclusion based on these discussions.* ✗

*. . . third, I will address the main concerns of the four stakeholders; **last,** I will offer a conclusion based on these discussions.* ✔

(See also 13.2.)

* * *

'Etc.' is short for 'et cetera' and means 'and the rest'/'and so forth'.

The meaning of the term implies 'and', so it does not need to come before it.

> *These include creativity, service, products, **and etc**.* ✗
>
> *These include creativity, service, products, **and e.t.c**.* ✗
>
> *These include creativity, service, products, **etc**.* ✔

Note that only one full stop is required—at the end.

REVEALED: 10.7 – *Whether to use 'no' or 'not' when forming negative sentences*

When a noun phrase is expressed in a negative manner, then 'no' should be used.

> *There is **not a** reason for this delay.* ✗
>
> *There is **no** reason for this delay.* ✔

> **!** When the sentence is expressing that something is not actually some-thing, then 'not a' can be used.
>
> *This is not a valid reason for withdrawing.*
>
> So,   *No reason = There aren't any possible 'reasons'.*
>
>   *Not a reason = This particular instance cannot be called a 'reason'*

For all other situations, 'not' is the correct term. In this next example an adjective is expressed negatively, so 'not' should be used.

> *This is **no** required for employees who have worked at the company for more than three years.* ✗
>
> *This is **not** required for employees who have worked at the company for more than three years.* ✔

10.8 Exercises

A. Which of the following are complete sentences (independent clauses), and which are incomplete/just additional information (dependent clauses)?

The collaboration was fairly successful _____

Since my colleagues were unwilling to change the topic _____

I made a suggestion about allocating tasks _____

Although there were times when the group fell silent _____

Without a coordinator in place during the meeting _____

B. Rewrite each of these incorrect sentences to make them error-free.

Naturally, greater the dose faster the medication will work.

_____

Not only the tutor should get involved but a member of the senior management.

_____

It is clear there is a component has not been fitted properly.

_____

C. For each sentence assess whether 'that' is required. Cross out the ones that can be omitted.

These employees worked in the department that was going to be restructured.

They knew that this was only a temporary measure.

The roles that they filled were quite varied.

The students were relieved that the exams were finally over.

Part B

Choices . . . to remember

11
NOUN-ADJECTIVE-VERB CONFUSION

Focus on . . . Noun-adjective differences

Noun-verb confusion

This chapter explores how related noun and adjective forms are misused, focusing initially on the typical endings or suffixes of these forms. Then the chapter addresses noun and verb confusion with a list that reveals the terms that prove particularly problematic to distinguish.

Background / 11.1 noun and adjective forms / 11.2 gender issues / 11.3 confusing pairs of nouns and verbs / 11.4 Exercises

Featured errors in 11:

see list (11.3) plus . . .
basic (11.1)
basis (11.1)
collectivism (11.1)
different (11.1)
economic (11.1)

economy (11.1)
interpretivist (11.1)
loose (11.3)
males (11.2)
minimalism (11.1)
rational (11.1)

significance (11.1)
strategic (11.1)
strategy (11.1)
woman (11.2)

BACKGROUND: Appreciating the difference between a noun and an adjective does not always prevent errors in written English. Often, familiarity is a better preventative tool. Suffixes can sometimes indicate the form of the word, for instance whether it is a noun or an adjective. Recognizing the common noun and adjective endings is one way to help eradicate this type of error.

The following sets of terms are commonly mixed up; writers use the noun form instead of the adjective, and vice versa. The noun forms end in *–nce*, and the adjective forms end in *–nt*.

Noun	Adjective	Noun	Adjective
absence	absent	confidence	confident
difference	different	distance	distant
dominance	dominant	importance	important
inconvenience	inconvenient	persistence	persistent
presence	present	prevalence	prevalent
prominence	prominent	relevance	relevant
silence	silent	tolerance	tolerant

 Not all adjectives end in *–nt* and not all words that end in *–nt* are adjectives.

*The **assistant** was there to gain experience of this type of environment.*

*An **incident** did occur when one of the assistants referred to a pupil as an **adolescent**.*

The three words ending in *–nt* in the above examples are nouns.

REVEALED: 11.1 – *How to distinguish the noun from its adjective form*

To avoid this very common error, it is important that the writer first stops to consider whether the noun or the adjective is required and then, if applicable, selects a term using the general *–nce* and *–nt* pattern mentioned above.

*This makes it difficult to detect small but potentially **significance** differences across groups.* ✗

*This makes it difficult to detect small but potentially **significant** differences across groups.* ✔

*The only **different** is that the first design used a hybrid material.* ✗

*The only **difference** is that the first design used a hybrid material.* ✔

* * *

In the social sciences, the suffix *–ism* is used frequently for nouns that name ideas or practices.

> **Positivism** *is a systematic, scientific, and objective-based approach to conducting research.*

Some of these nouns have adjective forms that end in *–ist*.

> *A **positivist** approach for this type of research has been suggested by Cheung (2000) and Morgan (2003).*

But people can also be labelled with this *–ist* suffix, and the term would then naturally be a noun.

> *He would also regard himself as a **positivist**, and his research certainly conforms to **positivist** paradigms.*

In the sentence above, the first instance of 'positivist' is a noun and the second is an adjective. These next examples demonstrate the *–ist* or *–ism* dilemma.

> *In a **collectivism** culture, people will value the interests of the social group more than they value individual interests.* ✗

> *In a **collectivist** culture, people will value the interests of the social group more than they value individual interests.* ✔

> *This research takes the position of **interpretivist**.* ✗

> *This research takes the position of **interpretivism**.* ✔

> *She was primarily a **minimalism** artist.* ✗

> *She was primarily a **minimalist** artist.* ✔

|➤ **RELATED ERRORS:**

Four sets of terms that cause noun-adjective confusion are presented here.

basic   adjective: essential; underlying
basis   noun: the main principle, the foundation

> The ***basic*** *of this is that reliable criteria will eventually be found.* ✘
>
> The ***basis*** *of this is that reliable criteria will eventually be found.* ✔

> *This is a **basis** principle in the area of fluid mechanics.* ✘
>
> *This is a **basic** principle in the area of fluid mechanics.* ✔

rational   adjective: reasonable, sensible
rationale   noun: the main reason accounting for something

Usually the noun 'rationale' is required.

> *The **rational** is that students will retain the information.* ✘
>
> *The **rationale** is that students will retain the information.* ✔

economy   noun: the way that money, businesses, and products are organized in
              a particular country, area, etc.
economic adjective: relating to business, industry, and managing money

> *The full effect is present in this particular country's **economic**.* ✘
>
> *The full effect is present in this particular country's **economy**.* ✔

> *There are different **economy** and political issues.* ✘
>
> *There are different **economic** and political issues.* ✔

strategy   noun: the set of plans and skills used in order to gain success or
              achieve an aim
strategic adjective: done as part of a military, business, or political plan

> *This will help to establish the best **strategic**.* ✘
>
> *This will help to establish the best **strategy**.* ✔

> *There is a need for **strategy** thinking here.* ✘
>
> *There is a need for **strategic** thinking here.* ✔

REVEALED: 11.2 – *When to use the noun and adjective forms for gender*

When using 'men' / 'women' and 'males' / 'females', the terms need to be consistent in the sentence (i.e., a noun should not be used for one gender and an adjective for the other).

*There were thirteen **males** and eleven women in total.* ✗

*There were thirteen **men** and eleven women in total.* ✔

And when writing generally, the terms should be either singular or plural (plural is usually appropriate for a general reference).

*Men are more likely to reject advice in this situation than is a **woman**.* ✗

*Men are more likely to reject advice in this situation than are **women**.* ✔

'Male' and 'female' can be adjectives or nouns, but as nouns ('a male', 'a female') they usually refer to animals; 'man' and 'woman' are preferred for humans in a study.

One man and three women were selected for this stage.

One male and three females were used to determine whether rats also have this ability.

REVEALED: 11.3 – *Noun and verb forms that attract errors*

Noun and verb forms can also generate errors. The following are particularly misused in sentences.

to adjust: verb   **adjustment**: noun

*This supported the **adjust** to the measures of the policy.* ✗

*This supported the **adjustment** to the measures of the policy.* ✔

to advise: verb   **advice**: noun

*The **advise** helped me to uncover more facts surrounding the investigation.* ✗

*The **advice** helped me to uncover more facts surrounding the investigation.* ✔

The tutor was there to *advice* the participants on how to use the program effectively. ✗

The tutor was there to *advise* the participants on how to use the program effectively. ✔

> As mentioned in 1.1, 'advice' is an uncountable noun so has no plural form and cannot be used with an indefinite article.
>
> *I would like to thank them for their effort and constant advices.* ✗
> *I would like to thank them for their effort and constant advice.* ✔
> *An advice that was given to me was to prepare thoroughly.* ✗
>
> A quantity phrase can be used instead: *A piece of advice . . .*

to analyse: verb   **analysis**: noun

Using frequency to analysis the condition helps in understanding which factors have a greater influence. ✗

Using frequency to analyse the condition helps in understanding which factors have a greater influence. ✔

Finally, there is an analyse of Chinese listed companies. ✗

Finally, there is an analysis of Chinese listed companies. ✔

> Note how the plural noun form is the same as the present tense of the verb.
>
> *These analyses should reveal where the problem is located.*
> *The computer analyses this data and then produces a report.*

to argue: verb   **argument**: noun

This argue had been raised on a number of occasions. ✗

This argument had been raised on a number of occasions. ✔

to believe: verb   **belief**: noun

> They *belief* this can only be achieved with further investment. ✘
> They ***believe*** this can only be achieved with further investment. ✔

> This is to assess the *believes* of the respondents. ✘
> This is to assess the ***beliefs*** of the respondents. ✔

(See also 1.3.)

to choose: verb   **choice**: noun

> It is a difficult *choose* for the policymakers. ✘
> It is a difficult ***choice*** for the policymakers. ✔

to complain: verb   **complaint**: noun

> Participant 3 also *complaints* about the amount of training provided. ✘
> Participant 3 also ***complains*** about the amount of training provided. ✔

> This is a common *complain* among the staff. ✘
> This is a common ***complaint*** among the staff. ✔

to examine: verb   **exam**: noun

> The next stage is to *exam* all the evidence collected so far. ✘
> The next stage is to ***examine*** all the evidence collected so far. ✔

to extend: verb   **extent**: noun

> The *extend* of this problem can be seen from the statistics below. ✘
> The ***extent*** of this problem can be seen from the statistics below. ✔

> It is not really known *to what extend* they differ from the normal population. ✘
> It is not really known ***to what extent*** they differ from the normal population. ✔

to lose: verb   **loss**: noun

> The downside to this is that they may *loss* some service. ✘
> The downside to this is that they may ***lose*** some service. ✔

*This is a great **lose** for the company.* ✘
*This is a great **loss** for the company.* ✔

The plural noun is 'losses'. There is a temptation to use the verb.

*This was a direct result of the **loses** made by the company in the previous year.* ✘
*This was a direct result of the **losses** made by the company in the previous year.* ✔

▷ RELATED ERRORS:

The verb is sometimes confused with the unrelated adjective 'loose'.

*In this case they may **loose** sensation in their fingers.* ✘
*In this case they may **lose** sensation in their fingers.* ✔

*This appears next to the **lose** material that had been used for a previous project.* ✘
*This appears next to the **loose** material that had been used for a previous project.* ✔

to participate: verb   **participant**: noun

*The next stage was to ask the **participates** to evaluate the three designs in front of them.* ✘

*The next stage was to ask the **participants** to evaluate the three designs in front of them.* ✔

to prove: verb   **proof**: noun

*This model **proofs** that external shocks have an important effect.* ✘
*This model **proves** that external shocks have an important effect.* ✔

*It is a **prove** of how much development is still required.* ✘
*It is **proof** of how much development is still required.* ✔

to pursue: verb   **pursuit**: noun

*The reason is that they **pursuit** this power as soon as they can.* ✘
*The reason is that they **pursue** this power as soon as they can.* ✔

to respond: verb   **response**: noun

> *Organizations need to **response** better to different strategic and business scenarios.* ✘
>
> *Organizations need to **respond** better to different strategic and business scenarios.* ✔

> *They were still waiting for a **respond** . . .* ✘
>
> *They were still waiting for a **response** . . .* ✔

> ❗ People who respond to a survey or questionnaire are 'respondents' not 'responds'.
>
> *There were five **responds** who were asked back for an interview.* ✘
>
> *There were five **respondents** who were asked back for an interview.* ✔

11.4 Exercises

A. Choose either the noun or the adjective form for each of these sentences.

There was no real different / difference between the two schemes.

Luo (1997) only looked at the figures that were important / importance to the shareholders.

The present / presence of the senior management team seemed to affect the performance of the sales team on this task.

In positivism / positivist research, the researcher is interested in gaining knowledge.

B. How many noun-verb mistakes can be found in this extract?

> When the degradation in the value of silver is combined with the diminution of the quantity of it contained in the coin of the same denomination, the lose is frequently still greater.

It was Adam Smith's believe that striving for personal gain is a natural human trait. Smith also proofed a number of other theories of the time, and the extend of his influence is still apparent today. Given its economy relevance, the argue put forward about the 'invisible hand' should be explored in more detail, and therefore a discussion will take place in the chapter that follows.

C. Select appropriate gender terms for each sentence.

man   men   woman   women   male   female   males   females

The aim was to interview at least three _____ and two _____ from each department.

One _____ rat was withdrawn from the process on account of its size.

_____ deaths were much lower for period four.

The number of _____ improving remained stable.

_____ are more likely to seek treatment early.

12
SELECTING THE CORRECT WORD

Focus on . . . Commonly confused terms

Prefixes

This chapter presents words that are commonly confused, including forms of the same root word. It also explores prefixes by first defining them and then explaining how the sentence structure can change when negative ones are applied.

Background / 12.1 commonly confused words /
12.2 prefix definitions and use / 12.3 Exercises

Featured errors in 12:

see list (12.1) plus . . .	existence (12.2)	no (12.2)
affected (12.2)	fairly (the same) (12.1)	not (12.2)
again (12.2)	fall (12.1)	other than (12.1)
almost (similar) (12.1)	inaccessible (12.2)	rather than (12.1)
assess (12.2)	inconsistent (12.2)	termed (12.1)
consistent (12.2)	named (12.1)	uneasy (12.2)

BACKGROUND: A similarity in spelling or sound or a similarity in meaning usually causes the following words, listed alphabetically, to be among the most likely to be confused by writers.

REVEALED: 12.1 – *Sets of words that are commonly confused*

about/regarding

> ***About*** *the third series, they note that it was largely affected by the limitations of the ADF test.* ✗

> ***Regarding*** *the third series, they note that it was largely affected by the limitations of the ADF test.* ✔   (See also 8.7.)

affect/effect

> *This had no **affect** on the results.* ✗
> *This had no **effect** on the results.* ✔

In the example above, 'effect' means result or consequence.

'Affect' is a verb meaning to have an influence on.

> *This may **effect** the company in the long term.* ✗
> *This may **affect** the company in the long term.* ✔

> 'Effect' is also a verb meaning 'to accomplish' or 'to bring about'.
>
> *This **affected** the change to wireless technology.* ✗
> *This **effected** the change to wireless technology.* ✔
>
> It is more commonly used as a noun, though.

apart from/except for

'Except for' excludes something or someone.

> *All regions were making a profit, **except for** the South West.*

'Apart from' can exclude OR include something or someone.

Apart from *philosophy, he has written on biology and linguistics.* (include)

*They discussed all the factors **apart from** the political ones.* (exclude)

The error is made when trying to use 'except for' to include something.

Except for *being an accountant, they have also been a media consultant and a salesperson.* ✘

Apart from *being an accountant, they have also been a media consultant and a salesperson.* ✔

> **!** Be careful when using 'for' and 'from' in these expressions:
>
> *... except from ... apart for*
>
> *... except for ... apart from*

as well/also

The first thing to note is that 'as well' is always two words (NOT *aswell*). It also normally goes at the end of a sentence.

*It could play an important part **as well.***

It can only go at the beginning in the form of 'As well as ...'.

As well as *leaving the company in debt, it damaged the reputation of the senior staff.*

'Also' can appear at the beginning of a sentence as a conjunctive adverb.

As well, there was very little funding available at the time. ✘

Also, *there was very little funding available at the time.* ✔

'Also' is often used before a verb.

*This could **as well** affect the reputations of the companies.* ✘

*This could **also** affect the reputations of the companies.* ✔

casual/causal

The first term means relaxed and unconcerned; the second relates to a cause.

> *These reforms weaken the argument that suggests there is a strong **casual** relation.* ✘
>
> *These reforms weaken the argument that suggests there is a strong **causal** relation.* ✔

called/known as

Only 'known' can be followed by 'as'.

> *This kind of software package is **known as** PFM software.*
>
> *Customers who buy online are called **as** e-customers.* ✘

The same rule applies to 'named' and 'termed'. They should not be followed by 'as'.

> *They are influenced by a set of factors—which Leung named **as** motivation factors.* ✘
>
> *These early phases are often termed **as** 'technology development'.* ✘

concern/consider

The verb 'to concern' has two primary meanings.

to relate to

> *This section **concerns** the problems they were facing at the time.*

to trouble or worry

> *They were **concerned about** this information being made available to the shareholders.*

But it is overused and misused by writers. It cannot be used in the following ways:

> *Tan et al. (2006) **concern** such a relationship the other way round.* ✘
>
> *Tan et al. (2006) **consider/view** such a relationship the other way round.* ✔
>
> *Both reliability and validity were **concerned** when analysing the results.* ✘
>
> *Both reliability and validity were **considered** when analysing the results.* ✔

*An inductive study tends to **concern** more on context.* ✘

*An inductive study tends to **concentrate/focus** more on context.* ✔

*They must **concern** at the reasons why this is taking place.* ✘

*They must **look** at the reasons why this is taking place.* ✔

*This paper has **concerned on** the reasons for the poor performance of the company.* ✘

*This paper has **examined/investigated** the reasons for the poor performance of the company.* ✔

contrary to/in contrast

Contrasting can be a complicated business. Three phrases can be employed.

On the contrary, *the United States failed to even consider this.*

In contrast, *the social world of business and management is complex.*

Contrary to *the findings in the journal, they found no instances at all.*

There is little difference between them, but 'in contrast' is normally used as a mere comparison. The other two ('on the contrary'/'contrary to') clearly state the opposite and show disagreement.

'On the contrary' can only be used as a response to something just mentioned.

On the contrary to the findings in the journal … ✘

The findings are not disappointing in this instance. ***On the contrary***, *they provide a number of …* ✔

In the contrary ✘   **On the contrary** ✔

In the contrast ✘   **In contrast** ✔

In contrary to ✘   **Contrary to** ✔

follow(ing)/as follows

The root word 'follow' and its various forms cause countless problems for writers.

*An estimation of the cost will also **follows**.*	**follow**
*… will be explained in the **follow** parts:*	**following**
*The advantages are described **as following**:*	**as follows**

*The three recommendations **as follows** a brief analysis.*	***follow***
*The **followings** are some suggestions:*	***following***

lack/fail

A distinction can be made between these two verbs.

to lack   verb: to be without

to fail   verb: to fall short in achieving something

*This still **lacks to explain** why they did not respond to the original supplement.* ✘

*This still **fails to explain** why they did not respond to the original supplement.* ✔

'Fail' is also mistakenly used instead of 'fall'.

*This is ignored as it **fails** outside the range.* ✘

*This is ignored as it **falls** outside the range.* ✔

|➤ RELATED ERRORS:

The verb and noun forms of 'lack' are often misused. A common error is using 'of' with the verb.

*Most lack **of** a suitable support network to deal with the implementation of new ICT.* ✘

*Most **lack a** suitable support network to deal with the implementation of new ICT.* ✔

It is the noun form that partners 'of'.

*There was a **lack of** motivation in many of the subjects.*

There is a tendency for the verb to be overlooked. Here is another example of a writer using the noun phrase by mistake.

*China still **lack of** research examining this inequality across provinces.* ✘

*China still **lacks** research examining this inequality across provinces.* ✔

rarely/merely

These adverbs may sound similar, but they have very little in common semantically.

rarely   adverb: seldom, infrequently

> *In fact, this system is **rarely** used as it is quite complex.*

merely   adverb: simply, only

> *The study based the selection criteria of participants **merely** on the research aims.*
> *Teachers **merely** have the opportunity to give SEN students their full attention.* ✗
> *Teachers **rarely** have the opportunity to give SEN students their full attention.* ✔

remain/keep

'Remain' and 'keep' are similar in meaning, and either can be used in this example.

> *It is crucial to **keep/remain** calm when this occurs.*

to remain   verb: to continue to be; to be left; to stay there

to keep   verb: to hold or retain; to maintain

When the meaning relates to something that continues to be or continues to exist, then 'remain' is the correct word.

> *This can **keep** a problem for those with learning difficulties.* ✗
> *This can **remain** a problem for those with learning difficulties.* ✔

'Keep' or 'retain' is required when the meaning relates to maintaining or holding on to something.

> *They need to **remain** their competitiveness for as long as possible.* ✗
> *They need to **keep/retain** their competitiveness for as long as possible.* ✔

remark/remind

> *This respondent also **reminded** that there are no guidelines currently in place.* ✗
> *This respondent also **remarked** that there are no guidelines currently in place.* ✔

rest/remaining

'Rest' and 'remaining' are terms that have similar meanings, so choosing between them is troublesome for many writers. There are, however, a few useful situations where one should be employed and the other rejected.

If a specific number is given, then 'rest' is not appropriate.

> **The rest 30** *cannot be detected at this stage.* ✘
>
> **The rest** *cannot be detected at this stage.* ✔

The following options are also available:

> *The* **remaining** *30/The* **other** *30 cannot be detected at this stage.*

'Rest' is a noun, and 'remaining' is an adjective. The nouns in these examples require 'remaining' to describe them.

> **The rest** *transformers supply the 33kV busbar.* ✘
>
> **The remaining** *transformers supply the 33kV busbar.* ✔

> *We will now look* **at the rest** *security goals.* ✘
>
> *We will now look at* **the remaining** *security goals.* ✔

The noun 'rest' cannot be used as a plural.

> **The rests** *were deemed unnecessary for what we are trying to achieve.* ✘
>
> **The rest** *were deemed unnecessary for what we are trying to achieve.* ✔

> | Whatever 'rest' is referring to will determine whether the verb is singular or plural.
>
> *The rest (of the evidence)* **is** *considered weak.*
> *The rest (of the users)* **were** *given a different task.*

rise/raise

to rise   verb: to increase

noun: an increase; an act of rising

to raise   verb: to lift up; to elevate

noun: an increase in amount (especially salary)

'Raise' as a verb always has an object linked to it.

*They **raised the level of payments** to three hundred dollars.*

'Rise' as a verb is used on its own and does not require a direct object.

*The prices will **rise** again in the future.*

As a rule, someone 'raises' something, but something 'rises'.

'Rise' is an irregular verb.

Present simple:

I/you/we/they	**rise**
he/she/it	**rises**
Present participle:	**rising**
Past participle:	**risen**
Past simple:	**rose**

Often the wrong verb or verb form is selected.

*In 2011, the number of companies **raised** to 24%.* ✗
*In 2011, the number of companies **rose** to 24%.* ✔

*They **rose** the price to coincide with this event.* ✗
*They **raised** the price to coincide with this event.* ✔

same/similar

same (as)   adjective: identical

similar   adjective: having a likeness or resemblance, especially in a general way

Note the article use.

*These figures were **the similar** as the previous ones.* ✗
*These figures were **the same** like the previous ones.* ✗
*These figures were **the same as** the previous ones.* ✔
OR: *These figures were **similar to** the previous ones.* ✔

Mistakes frequently occur when writers state that something is identical (*same*), when they actually just want to say there are some things in common (*similar*).

A same finding was reported by Cho (2009). ✗

A similar finding was reported by Cho (2009). ✔

Or: ***The same finding** was reported by Morgan (2009).* ✔

> **!** 'Same' is always used with a definite article.
>
> *The trade-off is that **the same** bank will also face losses.*

▷ RELATED ERRORS:

The phrases 'almost similar' and 'fairly the same' are incorrect.

*The communication outside the classroom will influence this level, which is **almost similar** to the social activities variable.* ✗

*The communication outside the classroom will influence this level, which is **similar to** the social activities variable.* ✔

*These findings are **fairly the same as** Cheng and Wang's.* ✗

*These findings are **similar to** Cheng and Wang's.* ✔

than/then

'Than' is a conjunction and is used to either introduce something that is in the lower degree or to compare generally.

'Then' is an adverb relating to time and means 'at that time' or 'after that'.

*This will also be much quicker **then** computer-based tasks.* ✗

*This will also be much quicker **than** computer-based tasks.* ✔

▷ RELATED ERRORS:

'Then' is also erroneously found in the following phrases:

*When applied to a sample of firms **other then** those used in developing the model, the results differ.* ✗

*When applied to a sample of firms **other than** those used in developing the model, the results differ.* ✔

*Research has looked at the causes of this **rather then** the effects on the population.* ✗

*Research has looked at the causes of this **rather than** the effects on the population.* ✔

trend/tend

'Trend' is a noun and means a general development or change in society. 'Tend' is a verb and means to behave in a certain way.

*These employees **trend** to perform a wider range of tasks.* ✗

*These employees **tend** to perform a wider range of tasks.* ✔

try/attempt

As a noun, 'try' cannot be used with the verb 'to make'. Instead, 'attempt' should be employed.

*A **try** was made to fix this problem before the third set of tests.* ✗

*An **attempt** was made to fix this problem before the third set of tests.* ✔

*They were **making a try** to distinguish between the two forms but unfortunately were let down by the data.* ✗

*They were **making an attempt** to distinguish between the two forms but unfortunately were let down by the data.* ✔

You can give something a try or have a try at something, but you 'make an attempt'.

underlying/underlining

'Underlining' relates to emphasis or actually drawing a line under something.

'Underlying' is an adjective and relates to something that is fundamental or something that is present but not obvious.

*Attention is paid to this subsystem in order to reveal **underlining** elements that disrupt stability.* ✗

*Attention is paid to this subsystem in order to reveal **underlying** elements that disrupt stability.* ✔

well/good

A person who is 'well' can also be 'good', so deciding between the two descriptive words can be a problem. In this instance (stating that someone is 'well'), 'well' is an adjective meaning healthy. But in academic writing its main use is as an adverb, and this is where the distinction from 'good' occurs. 'Good' is an adjective and therefore is mainly used with nouns to describe the subject of the sentence. It comes before the noun.

*There was **a well turnout**, and this contributed to the success of the evening.* ✘

*There was **a good turnout**, and this contributed to the success of the evening.* ✔

*In order to form **a well understanding**, both parts must be read.* ✘

*In order to form **a good understanding**, both parts must be read.* ✔

So if a noun is being described, then 'good' should be used.

'Well' often modifies a verb or adjective.

*They performed **good** in the second task.* ✘

*They performed **well** in the second task.* ✔

It only ever describes a noun when it is part of a compound adjective.

*He is a **well-behaved** pupil in the morning lessons.*

REVEALED: 12.2 – *How to use prefixes effectively*

A prefix is an element that is attached to the beginning of a word and serves to modify that word, creating a new one in the process. Each prefix has a specific meaning that can help with assessing the meaning of a term; however, it is not always obvious which prefix should be used in a given situation. These definitions offer some guidance.

de: take something away; do the opposite of; reduce   **dis**: reverse; opposite

dys: difficult; bad; abnormal   **hetero**: different

homo: same; alike   **hyper**: excessive; above

in: not, negative; into   **iso**: equal; same

mal: bad; abnormal   **mis**: bad, badly; wrong

non: not; absence of   **poly**: many

re: again; repeatedly   **un**: not; opposite (not always a negative meaning)

If there is an appropriate prefix that can be attached to a particular word, then it should be used. It is always preferable to adding 'not'or 'again'.

> Based on this they need to **assess again** the parameters ... ✗
>
> Based on this they need to **reassess** the parameters ... ✔

In this next example, the prefix 'non' should be adopted.

> The second respondent complained that the support for the department was almost **not existent**. ✗
>
> The second respondent complained that the support for the department was almost **no existence**. ✗
>
> The second respondent complained that the support for the department was almost **nonexistent**. ✔

A writer will sometimes be unsure about which prefix to use to create a negative meaning. Looking the form up in a dictionary to see if it exists is advisable.

> Critics argued that the system was **unaccessible** to most of the employees. ✗
>
> Critics argued that the system was **non-accessible** to most of the employees. ✗
>
> Critics argued that the system was **inaccessible** to most of the employees. ✔

> Words that contain negative prefixes are not always opposites of the positive form. For instance, 'uneasy' is not the opposite of 'easy'.
>
> Although the first group completed the task well, the third group found the task **uneasy**. ✗
>
> Although the first group completed the task well, the third group found the task **difficult**. ✔
>
> 'Uneasy' means troubled or uncomfortable.

Not using an available prefix is even more apparent when the sentence appears to begin in a positive way:

> This makes it ... (as opposed to 'This does not make it').

The reader is expecting the sentence to continue along these lines, but instead ...

> This makes it not a suitable case study to use.

A better option would be to use a prefix with a negative meaning so the sentence can retain its form without the need for 'not'.

> This makes it an **unsuitable** case study to use.

Sometimes a choice is available between a negative beginning to the sentence and a prefix indicating negation.

> All of the company's websites were **not affected**. ✘
>
> **None of** the company's websites were **affected**. ✔
>
> **All of** the company's websites were **unaffected**. ✔   (See also 3.5.)

|➤ **RELATED ERRORS:**

The terms 'consistent' and 'inconsistent' are often misused. The following construction is common:

> This is **in consistence** with Leung's proposal. ✘

Depending on the desired meaning the two options are:

> This is **consistent** with Leung's proposal. ✔
>
> This is **inconsistent** with Leung's proposal. ✔

12.3 Exercises

A. Select from the 'following' options and fill in the gaps.

follow   following   as follows   follows

This will be explained in the _____ parts:

The advantages are described _____:

The three recommendations _____ a brief analysis.

An estimation of the cost will also _____.

The _____ are some suggestions:

B. Cross out the incorrect option(s) for each sentence.

This will also rise/raise the price of the commodity in the short term.

The similar/same finding was reported by Chen (2009) and Tran (2013).

Some of the teachers concerned/considered/concentrated this measure and then agreed it could provide a solution to the problem.

The accuracy and the relevance of the content cannot be guaranteed, and this also/as well applies to any links that are provided on their pages.

C. Match the prefixes to the root words. One has already been done.

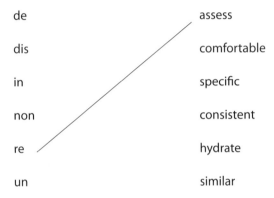

de   assess

dis   comfortable

in   specific

non   consistent

re   hydrate

un   similar

13
SELECTING THE CORRECT STYLE

Focus on . . . Unsuitable expressions

Unsuitable style

Redundant terms

Nominalization

This chapter examines language that is inappropriate for academic writing and reveals the individual terms that should be avoided. It explores adjective choice and how writing can be improved by removing unnecessary phrases from sentences, to improve clarity and understanding. It ends with a discussion on the merits of using noun phrases and verbs.

13.1 contractions / 13.2 phrases to avoid / 13.3 excessive adjectives / 13.4 clarity and redundancy in writing / 13.5 verbs in sequence / 13.6 nominalization / 13.7 Exercises

Featured errors in 13:

absolutely (13.3)	don't (13.1)	majorly (13.2)
afterwards (13.4)	each (13.4)	massive (13.3)
again (13.4)	extremely (13.3)	quit (13.2)
anyway (13.2)	few (13.4)	reckon (13.2)
as mentioned (13.4)	incredible (13.3)	return (13.4)
at last (13.2)	interconnected (13.4)	revise (13.4)
basically (13.2)	investigate (13.6)	totally (13.2)
brand new (13.4)	isn't (13.1)	very (13.3)
brief (13,4)	last but not least (13.2)	
continue (13.4)	magnificent (13.3)	

REVEALED: 13.1 – *When contractions are acceptable and when they should be avoided*

Some words can be shortened by using an apostrophe to replace missing letters, but this is only really acceptable in academic writing when transcribing interviews and directly quoting. In this next example it is inappropriate.

> *Investors **don't** have access to this type of information.* ✘
>
> *Investors **do not** have access to this type of information.* ✔

The contraction is not appropriate in the opening sentence of this next set, but it can be used when relaying exactly what a respondent has said.

> *Respondent D believed that this **wouldn't** address the needs of the community.* ✘
>
> *Respondent D believed that this **would not** address the needs of the community.* ✔
>
> *'We **haven't** been given a voice, and the decisions are being made without any input from the local people,' reiterated Respondent C.* ✔

REVEALED: 13.2 – *Which phrases to avoid in academic writing*

Some phrases are either too informal or not precise enough for academic writing. The following terms should be avoided:

Use 'however' or 'regardless', not 'anyway'.

> ***Anyway**, these factors will be addressed in the research.* ✘

Often there is no need to replace 'anyway' with another term, but sometimes 'however' or 'regardless' is appropriate.

> *There were also limited data available for India. **Anyway**, we decided to retain this country in our sample because ...* ✘
>
> *There were also limited data available for India; **however**, we decided to retain this country in our sample because ...* ✔

Use 'essentially' or 'ultimately', not 'basically'.

If an adverb must be used, then opt for 'essentially' or 'ultimately' instead.

> ***Basically***, *the money spent on this project was misused.* ✘
>
> ***Ultimately***, *the money spent on this project was misused.* ✔

Use 'last', not 'at last'. (See 10.6.)

Use 'last', not 'last but not least'.

'Last but not least' is a fixed phrase used to indicate that a final point is being made but is no less important than those preceding it. It should be avoided and replaced with simply 'last'.

> ***Last but not least***, *the overall conclusion will be presented in chapter eight.* ✘
>
> ***Last***, *the overall conclusion will be presented in chapter eight.* ✔

Use 'largely' / 'greatly', not 'majorly'.

'Majorly' is another word that crops up quite often but should be treated as informal and avoided. There are plenty of other adverbs to use in its place.

> *They ended up focusing* ***majorly*** *on how to improve the packaging of the product.* ✘
>
> *They ended up focusing* ***largely*** *on how to improve the packaging of the product.* ✔

> *This has* ***majorly*** *increased both the price and the production time.* ✘
>
> *This has* ***greatly*** *increased both the price and the production time.* ✔

Use 'withdraw', not 'quit'.

When referring to participants leaving a research study, the most suitable verb is 'to withdraw'.

> *In total, four patients* ***quit*** *the study before the second consultation meeting.* ✘
>
> *In total, four patients* ***withdrew from*** *the study before the second consultation meeting.* ✔

Opt for 'imagine', 'consider' or 'suppose' instead of 'reckon'.

> *They* ***reckon*** *it will be a lot smaller when the final design is presented.* ✘
>
> *They* ***imagine*** *it will be a lot smaller when the final design is presented.* ✔

Use 'in total', not 'totally'.

'Totally' is a more informal word for 'completely' but should be avoided in academic writing and used only for conversational pieces.

> *'Some of the material is **totally** biodegradable, but some of it is only partially,' revealed Interviewee C.*

It cannot be used as an alternative to 'in total'.

> *There were sixty participants **totally**.* ✘
>
> *There were **totally** sixty participants.* ✘
>
> *There were sixty participants **in total**.* ✔

REVEALED: 13.3 – *Adjectives and adverbs that are inappropriate or unnecessary*

Some writers make the mistake of using strong adjectives or inserting adverbs to try to convince the reader of something. Often this leads to overemphasis or exaggeration and gives the impression that the writer is trying too hard to persuade the reader. More modest adjectives and phrases can assist the writer in presenting a view or idea that the reader is more likely to accept.

> *An **incredible** observation is that once a patient has . . .* ✘
>
> *A **key** observation is that once a patient has . . .* ✔
>
> *It also led to a **magnificent** decrease in lost data.* ✘
>
> *It also led to a **marked** decrease in lost data.* ✔
>
> *There is a **massive** amount of research on this topic.* ✘
>
> *There is a **large/great** amount of research on this topic.* ✔

Some adjectives already have a strong meaning and therefore do not require any assistance from adverbs to add emphasis. These include 'crucial', 'critical', and 'necessary'.

> *This is **absolutely** crucial to the success of the scheme.* ✘
>
> *It is a **very** critical issue and one that will be addressed next.* ✘
>
> *Creating a detailed schedule for the field work is also **extremely** necessary.* ✘

REVEALED: 13.4 – *How to make writing clear and efficient*

Although identifying unnecessary phrases and eliminating wordiness can be a challenge, there are some terms that can be easily edited to reduce word count and avoid redundancy.

Based on what has been discussed above, *three hypotheses can be formed.* ✘

Based on the above (discussion)*, three hypotheses can be formed.* ✔

As it has been mentioned previously in this study, *the main development occurred in the 1960s.* ✘

As mentioned earlier*, the main development occurred in the 1960s.* ✔

This is a ***brand new*** *design and incorporates all these elements.* ✘

This is a ***new*** *design and incorporates all these elements.* ✔

These initial interviews were ***brief in duration*** *and only covered personal details.* ✘

These initial interviews were ***brief*** *and only covered personal details.* ✔

There are ***few in number*** *in this area of the college, and there have been complaints from some departments.* ✘

There are ***few*** *in this area of the college, and there have been complaints from some departments.* ✔

This ***continues to remain*** *an issue for students without a recognized teaching qualification.* ✘

This ***remains*** *an issue for students without a recognized teaching qualification.* ✔

The next stage is to ensure all the nodes are ***interconnected to each other****.* ✘

The next stage is to ensure all the nodes are ***interconnected****.* ✔

The frequency for this region was 400 cars ***per each*** *kilometre.* ✘

The frequency for this region was 400 cars ***per*** *kilometre.* ✔

➤ RELATED ERRORS:

The prefix *re–* means 'again', so it is usually unnecessary to add this or a similar word.

*The proposal was **revised again** to eliminate these inconsistencies.* ✘

*The proposal was **revised** to eliminate these inconsistencies.* ✔

*The report was **renamed afterwards** 'Effective Planning in Rural Conservation Areas'.* ✘

*The report was **renamed** 'Effective Planning in Rural Conservation Areas'.* ✔

*It would be useful to **return back** to the original question.* ✘

*It would be useful to **return** to the original question.* ✔

*   *   *

Repetition is also apparent when writers are introducing or naming something. Usually a second reference will not require the thing to be named in its entirety. Instead, shortening the terms or using pronouns can prevent needless repetition. These two examples will demonstrate the point. (See also 3.1.)

*The Gregory-Hansen linear cointegration model was applied initially. The **Gregory-Hansen linear cointegration model** is useful because it can . . .* ✘

*The Gregory-Hansen linear cointegration model was applied initially. The **model** is useful because it can . . .* ✔

*Using this tool can help analysts decide which routes **analysts** should take.* ✘

*Using this tool can help analysts decide which routes **they** should take.* ✔

REVEALED: 13.5 *– That verbs in a sequence are more effective than a mixture of verbs and nouns*

When listing a sequence of points, it is desirable to keep the format consistent. If the list begins with a verb, it is advisable to retain a parallel structure with all the verbs in the same form; mixing verbs and nouns in a list should also be avoided.

The purpose of the journal is to introduce the process, analysing the methods used and reflect on the outcomes. ✘

The purpose of the journal is to introduce the process, analyse the methods used and reflect on the outcomes. ✔

*The key steps involved analysing the problem, identifying a method, **application of** the chosen method . . .* ✘

*The key steps involved analysing the problem, identifying a method, **applying** the chosen method . . .* ✔

REVEALED: 13.6 – *What nominalization is and when it can be used*

Nominalization occurs when a verb (or adjective) is replaced by its related noun form. Sometimes it results in a weak and drawn-out sentence compared to its verb counterpart.

investigate: verb   **investigation**: noun

> *They investigated the resources available to international students.*
>
> *They carried out an investigation of the resources available to international students.*

Although the second example above is not grammatically incorrect, it is not efficient or particularly effective writing. But the nominalization in this next example would be considered ineffective.

> *They also looked at procedures **for an investigation of** the issue of plagiarism in the work of high school students.* ✗
>
> *They also looked at procedures **for investigating** the issue of plagiarism in the work of high school students.* ✔

But choosing verbs to form active voice (see 5.8) instead of using noun phrases is not always advisable. Inserting a noun phrase can add variety and prevent repetition, and it can provide a link to a previous idea or action. This next example is a bit repetitive with two identical verbs and two pronouns ('we'), whereas the noun phrase in the second example helps the writing to flow a bit better.

> *We discussed the optimum size of the network with the relevant managers. We also discussed key security features to ensure . . .*
>
> ***We discussed** the optimum size of the network with the relevant managers. **A discussion of the** key security features also took place to ensure . . .*

If the guidelines of a particular subject suggest avoiding 'we' (see 3B), then nominalization is one option available. The problem is that constant use can lead to undynamic passive writing and long-winded sentences. Notice in the examples above how nominalization requires extra phrases such as 'carried out' and 'also took place' to be present for the sentence to make sense and to be grammatical.

13.7 Exercises

A. Cross out the unnecessary words in this extract.

Returning back to the original design, it is very obvious that the brand new model created by Smith Motors is definitely the best. We then ranked the companies in the order Orion, Dubaki, Renton Spares. Last but not least is Spades, but they were hampered by crazy misfortune when their mechanic was taken ill; their design team was also comparatively small in number. This proved to be very critical, as Wu (2007) suggests that five members is optimal.

Based on the results that have been stated above, we conclude that . . .

B. What is a more appropriate term for each of these phrases?

majorly _____   wildly _____   reckon   _____

couldn't _____   at last _____   basically _____

Part C

Components . . . to review

14
REGIONS AND COUNTRIES

Focus on . . . Regions and countries as nouns

Regions and countries as adjectives

This chapter offers instruction on how to refer to countries and regions and how to recognize the differences between the noun and the adjective forms. It also addresses generic and specific sentences, the order of adjectives in a sentence with a country reference, and the capitalization of these terms.

Background / 14.1 countries as adjectives /
14.2 noun and adjective confusion / 14.3 order of adjectives /
14.4 Exercises

Featured errors in 14:

Asia/Asian (14.2, 14.3)
China/Chinese (14.1, 14.2)
Germany/German (14.2)
Hong Kong (14B)
India/Indian (14.2)

Japan/Japanese (14.2)
Korea/Korean (14.2)
UK (14B, 14.1)
US (14B)

BACKGROUND: Although most proper nouns do not require an article, the names of some countries and regions have 'the' as part of their name.

the United Kingdom   the People's Republic of China

the Netherlands   the United States

I will now compare the stock markets of UK and Hong Kong. For the reasons stated earlier, US and Japan will not be considered here. ✗

*I will now compare the stock markets of **the** UK and Hong Kong. For the reasons stated earlier, **the** US and Japan will not be considered here.* ✔

> **!** The correct form is 'Hong Kong', not any of the following:
>
> *Hong kong   Hongkong   HongKong   Hon Kong*

REVEALED: 14.1 – *Which forms to use when countries act as modifiers*

Despite the information provided about the UK and the US above, countries and regions that have 'the' as part of their name do not always have to be preceded by 'the'. When the country/region acts like an adjective in a noun phrase and that phrase has a generic meaning, then 'the' will not be required. (See also 2.3.)

***The UK economic growth** has yet to recover from the 2008 recession.* ✗

***UK economic growth** has yet to recover from the 2008 recession.* ✔

> **!** In the example above the UK is acting like an adjective. Its adjective form is the same as its noun form. Many countries have different forms for the name of the country and for the adjective of the country; for instance, 'Chinese economic growth' not 'China economic growth' would be used in the above situation.

In the example above, 'economic growth' is the subject and means economic growth of the UK in general. So 'the UK' loses its definite article. Here are two more examples to illustrate this point and a further one.

Chinese economy is gradually improving after the poorer than expected growth of last year. ✗

The Chinese economic growth *has yet to recover from . . .* ✗

The writer of the first example may have assumed that the reference was general (or has not realized that 'economy' might require an article because it is a singular countable noun) and therefore has not used an article. Similarly, the second example is referring to the economic growth of a particular country (China), and so the writer believes a definite article is needed.

However, in the first example the economy is the subject, and it is a countable noun so requires an article. In the second example 'economic growth' is the subject, and growth is taken to have a generic meaning (even though it relates to a specific country, China) so does not require an article. (See also 9.2.)

The Chinese economy *is gradually improving after the poorer than expected growth of last year.* ✔

Chinese economic growth *has yet to recover from these recent setbacks.* ✔

> **!** If this last example was rearranged into an 'of' phrase, an article would then be required.
>
> **The** *economic growth of China has yet to recover from these recent setbacks.*

In this next example, a particular (specific) industry is being referred to, so the definite article is warranted.

This has proven to be a real boost for **Chinese steel industry.** ✗

This has proven to be a real boost for **the Chinese steel industry.** ✔

REVEALED: 14.2 – *How to recognize the adjective form and the noun form of countries and their people*

Adjectives and nouns are often confused (see 11.1), and this is certainly true when countries and their people are being referenced. As touched upon earlier, this first example will require the adjective form.

*The current **China government** promotes economic growth and prioritizes money before environmental problems.* ✘

*The current **Chinese government** promotes economic growth and prioritizes money before environmental problems.* ✔

Regardless of whether they are nouns or adjectives, all terms derived from countries must begin with a capital letter.

*This is a typical experience for a **Chinese** student living abroad.*

***China** and **South Korea** have yet to release their figures.*

In this next example the writer is naming countries so nouns are needed, not adjectives.

*Future studies could assess similar methodologies with the data of multiple countries such as **Korean, Japanese**, and China.* ✘

*Future studies could assess similar methodologies with the data of multiple countries such as **Korea, Japan**, and China.* ✔

Care must also be taken with the noun and adjective forms 'Asia' and 'Asian'.

*It means that other **Asia** countries are able to sell products of similar quality.* ✘

*It means that other **Asian** countries are able to sell products of similar quality.* ✔

*In order to understand inter-regionalism between **Asian** and Europe, it is necessary to study how the regions are constructed.* ✘

*In order to understand inter-regionalism between **Asia** and Europe, it is necessary to study how the regions are constructed.* ✔

* * *

When introducing a list of places as 'countries', naturally there should not be any regions or continents in it.

*The **countries** that will adopt this include Japan, China, Europe, and the US.* ✘

*The **regions** that will adopt this include Japan, China, Europe, and the US.* ✔

*The countries that will adopt this include Japan, China, and the US. **Europe** is also set to introduce . . .* ✔

* * *

The noun and the adjective forms of some nations and their people are listed here with associated errors.

noun	adjective	noun	adjective	noun	adjective
Germany	German	France	French	Switzerland	Swiss
India	Indian	Japan	Japanese	Thailand	Thai
Malaysia	Malaysian	Taiwan	Taiwanese	Brazil	Brazilian

*The study took place in **German** and France.* ✗

*The study took place in **Germany** and France.* ✔

*Twenty **India participants** were selected for stage one.* ✗

*Twenty **Indian participants** were selected for stage one.* ✔

Note that nouns that name the language of a country have the same form as the country's adjective.

***German** is also spoken in this region.*

*For these students the questionnaire was also written in **Chinese**.*

REVEALED: 14.3 – *How to order adjectives that contain a country reference*

The order of adjectives needs to be recognized when there is more than one describing a noun. The adjective for nationality should come after other modifiers (and therefore be nearest the noun).

*This is an **Asian small country** located on the same peninsular.* ✗

*This is a **small Asian country** located on the same peninsular.* ✔

*The **Taiwanese emerging market** will no doubt play a part in the near future.* ✗

*The **emerging Taiwanese market** will no doubt play a part in the near future.* ✔

14.4 Exercises

A. Select either the adjective or the noun for each sentence.

We interviewed three Germany/German employees, two Korea/Korean employees, and the manager of the company (who was born in Germany/German) at the Japan/Japanese headquarters in Tokyo.

A number of China/Chinese firms have been studied, two from the north of China/Chinese and three from the south. We also discuss the findings of Yoshinaga (2009), who looked at the performance of Japan/Japanese firms listed on Japan's/Japan/Japanese stock exchange.

B. How many of these sentences contain incorrect references to a country, nationality, or language? Cross out the error(s) and insert the correction(s) in the space provided.

They identified how the China government can resolve this issue. _____

We focus on the UK, the US, Germany, and France. _____

China economy is beginning to emerge from the crisis. _____

France steel companies have not suffered the same fate as their counterparts in the UK. _____

We looked at the structure of the following languages: Korea, Japanese, Germany, English, and French. _____

15

DATES AND TIME EXPRESSIONS

Focus on . . . Dates

Expressions of time

This chapter focuses on using dates and selecting appropriate time phrases for particular situations. It covers general formatting, prepositional selection, and the relevant tense to use. It also explains how certain expressions can date events in sequence.

Featured errors in 15:

from (15.4)	on (15.2)
less than (15.4)	recent decades (15.3)
in (15.2)	since (15.4)
nowadays (15.6)	until (15.4)

REVEALED: 15.1 – *How to write dates correctly*

It is increasingly common for dates to be written without an apostrophe if there is no possession taking place.

*This style of clothing was typical in the **1970s**.*

But the normal rules apply when there is possession.

*I will concentrate on **1970s'** fashion and the way the music scene influenced these designs.*

 Some tutors might prefer this last example to be rephrased rather than using a possessive apostrophe.

I will concentrate on the fashion of the 1970s and the way the music scene influenced these designs.

Avoid the definite article when referring to a year.

*In **the** 2012, a number of protests took place in the town square.* ✘

When the year acts like an adjective to refer to an event, the article is needed.

They were present at the 2012 Health Education Conference.

Dates must always be written in numbers, not in words.

*The technology was available in the **nineteen eighties**, but there was no way to apply it.* ✘

*The technology was available in the **1980s**, but there was no way to apply it.* ✔

REVEALED: 15.2 – *Which prepositions to use with dates*

There are a few general rules about when to use 'in' and 'on' with dates.

'In' is used for months and years.

*This occurred **in** June.*

*This occurred **in** June 2004.*

*This occurred **in** 2009.*

*The data was collected **on** March 2010.* ✘

*The data was collected **in** March 2010.* ✔

And 'on' is used for specific dates and days of the week.

*This occurred **on** June 15th, 2004.*

*This occurred **on** Tuesday.*

*This occurred **in** 4th October.* ✘

*This occurred **on** 4th October.* ✔

REVEALED: 15.3 – *Which tense to use when mentioning the date of something*

Most of the time writers will be referring to studies or events that have taken place in the past. When providing a past date, the tense needs to reflect this.

*In 2010 they **are** faced with a similar situation.* ✘

*In 2010 they **were** faced with a similar situation.* ✔

Equally, when a future date is mentioned, the tense has to match.

*The next conference **took place** in Beijing in 2019.* ✘

*The next conference **will take place** in Beijing in 2019.* ✔

If the date of an event or research paper is the same as the year in which the work is being written (2016 below), then the present perfect or simple past is normally appropriate when referring to it.

*The situation was bound to escalate, and 2016 **has seen** renewed fighting in the region.*

*In 2016 they **began** testing this device over small areas.*

▷ **RELATED ERRORS:**

'Recent years' is a better term than 'recent decades'. Given the fast-changing nature of industry and research, there is nothing 'recent' about 20 or 30 years ago. 'Past few' can be used for decades and the sentence written in the present perfect.

> *As a key component of many economic activities, the demand for radio spectrum* **is** *rising in recent years.* ✘

> *As a key component of many economic activities, the demand for radio spectrum* **has been** *rising in recent years.* ✔

> *There* **was** *an increase in capability in the past few decades, and this has resulted in . . .* ✘

> *There* **has been** *an increase in capability in the past few decades, and this has resulted in . . .* ✔

REVEALED: 15.4 – *Which phrases to use for certain time periods*

Selecting the correct expression for time periods can be confusing. The following chart shows the start and end points for the key terms.

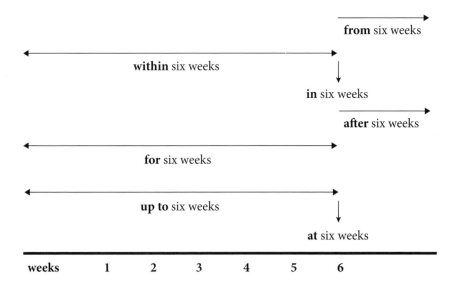

Time prepositions are some of the hardest to comprehend; fortunately, there are certain ones that can be defined and distinguished.

'Until' is used when the activity continues up to a specific end point.

*We will continue **until** there are no more outliers left.*

'By' can be used to set a time limit for an activity or situation.

*The effects should be known **until** 18:00.* ✘

*The effects should be known **by** 18:00.* ✔ ('by 18:00' means no later than 18:00)

* * *

Another pair of time prepositions is 'since' and 'from'. These two terms can be distinguished as follows:

'From' can be used to indicate a specific time as a starting point in the future.

***Since 2018**, this will be made compulsory for all workers.* ✘

***From 2018,** this will be made compulsory for all workers.* ✔

'Since' can be used for an event beginning in the past and still continuing today.

From 1999, this has been the responsibility of the Ministry of Home Affairs. ✘

***Since 1999**, this has been the responsibility of the Ministry of Home Affairs.* ✔

'From' can also indicate the first of two specific points (with 'to' or 'until').

*The session took place **from** 6:00 until 7:00.*

▷ RELATED ERRORS:

Recognizing the context is important when choosing between 'less than' and 'up to'. These terms do not express the same time frame because technically 'up to six months' could be the whole six months, whereas 'less than six months' cannot be as long as six months. Errors occur when the writer wishes to imply that the length of time is long or excessive (i.e., a negative connotation); 'less than' would then be inappropriate.

Given the alterations that have been identified, the finished model may even take **less than** *two years to build.* ✘

Given the alterations that have been identified, the finished model may even take **up to** *two years to build.* ✔

A crime of this severity will carry a sentence of **less than** *15 years.* ✘

A crime of this severity will carry a sentence of **up to** *15 years.* ✔

REVEALED: 15.5 *– How to form time phrases that are adjectives modifying a noun*

When time phrases represent an adjective modifying a noun, the unit of time needs to be in the singular form and the term hyphenated.

This **three years cycle** *was confirmed by the research group in 1967.* ✘

This **three-year cycle** *was confirmed by the research group in 1967.* ✔

A **twenty minutes break** *every three hours is now recommended for jobs of this nature.* ✘

A **twenty-minute break** *every three hours is now recommended for jobs of this nature.* ✔

(See also 9.2.)

REVEALED: 15.6 *– The difference between 'today' and 'nowadays'*

Writers often use 'nowadays' and 'today' interchangeably, but they have different uses.

The only time they do have similar purposes is when starting a sentence in the following way:

Today/Nowadays, these areas are much more tightly controlled as a result of . . .

In the example above, 'today' does not refer to 'this day' but takes on the meaning of 'at the current time'.

The mistake occurs when writers try to give 'nowadays' possession. Nowadays can only be used as an adverb and therefore cannot take a possessive form like 'today' can.

> In **nowaday's** market, it is important to take advantage of investment from these new online sources. ✘

> In **today's** market, it is important to take advantage of investment from these new online sources. ✔

To use nowadays here it must be rephrased.

> In the market **nowadays** . . .

That said, 'nowadays' might be considered too informal for some situations. Terms such as 'today', 'current', and 'contemporary' have a more academic sound to them.

> In the **current** market . . .

15.7 Exercises

A. How many mistakes are there in the following passage? Rewrite the passage in the lines provided.

Since 2020 the headquarters will be in Munich. This move has come about because of nowaday's market, where production is centring on Germany. On June the company issued a statement detailing the move and that within three years they wanted to streamline the business prior to relocation on 2020. In recent years profits were declining, so action needed to be taken.

_____

_____

_____

_____

B. Fill in the gaps with either 'since' or 'from'.

The government has been discussing this _____ Tuesday.

This has only been happening _____ the new software was installed.

The measures will hopefully be in place _____ Tuesday.

The office is open _____ 9:00 until 12:00 noon at the weekend.

C. Cross out the phrases that are unsuitable, based on the information provided. The first one has been done for you.

It should not take as long as six weeks.

~~from six weeks~~   within six weeks   ~~in six weeks~~   ~~after six weeks~~
~~for six weeks~~   up to six weeks   ~~at six weeks~~

It is likely to take longer than six weeks.

from six weeks   within six weeks   in six weeks   after six weeks
for six weeks   up to six weeks   at six weeks

It is likely to last six weeks.

from six weeks   within six weeks   in six weeks   after six weeks
for six weeks   up to six weeks   at six weeks

It will start around six weeks' time.

from six weeks   within six weeks   in six weeks   after six weeks
for six weeks   up to six weeks   at six weeks

16
NUMBERS AND PERCENTAGES

Focus on . . . Numbers

Rank and order

Percentages

This chapter focuses on numbers and percentages and covers the issues of format, use, and suitability of terms. It also addresses the differences between cardinal and ordinal numbers and how to express fractions correctly.

16.1 using numbers / 16.2 order of adjectives / 16.3 ordinal numbers / 16.4 rank and article use / 16.5 fractions / 16.6 prepositional choice / 16.7 working with percentages / 16.8 Exercises

Featured errors in 16:

additional (16.2)
divided by (16.6)
double (16.5)
eight (16.3)
eleventh (16.3)
equals (16.6)
fewer than (16.7)
first (16.2, 16.4)
fourth (16.3)
fortieth (16.3)

forty (16.3)
fourteen (16.3)
hundred (16.1)
last (16.2)
less than (16.7)
main (16.2)
million (16.1)
next (16.2)
percent/percentage
  (16.7)

quarters (16.5)
rank (16.3)
second (16.3, 16.4)
seventeenth (16.3)
thirds (16.5)
thousand (16.1)
twelfth (16.3)
twice (16.5)

REVEALED: 16.1 – *How to use numbers in a sentence*

Numbers should only be spelled out using letters if they are under 11.

> The aim was to have at least **one hundred and twenty-five** questionnaires returned by the end of week six. ✘
>
> The aim was to have at least **125** questionnaires returned by the end of week six. ✔

> ❗ If a number begins the sentence, then it must be spelled out regardless of its value.
>
> *14 theories have been offered, and these will be evaluated next.* ✘
>
> **Fourteen** *theories have been offered, and these will be evaluated next.* ✔
>
> *3 steel frames were acquired from Danvers, a local company.* ✘
>
> **Three** *steel frames were acquired from Danvers, a local company.* ✔

Numbers, not words, should always be used with units.

> The guidelines suggest that this should be a **fifteen cm** incision. ✘
>
> The guidelines suggest that this should be a **15 cm** incision. ✔

Numbers and letters should not be mixed when writing out a number. This is commonly seen with hundreds and thousands.

> The government is hoping the scheme will create **150 thousand** new jobs. ✘
>
> The government is hoping the scheme will create **150,000** new jobs. ✔

> ❗ When spelling out exact numbers, 'hundred', 'thousand', and 'million' should not be made plural even if their unit value is more than one.
>
> *Three* **thousands** *are used with this device.* ✘
>
> *Three* **thousand** *are used with this device.* ✔

|➤ RELATED ERRORS:

When separating thousands and hundreds of thousands, a comma should be used and not a decimal point.

3.500   200.000   **3,500   200,000**

REVEALED: 16.2 *– How to sequence adjectives that include a number*

When used alongside adjectives to modify a noun, the placement of the number is important. The number must go after sequence words such as 'first', 'next', and 'last'.

The **three next cases** relate to the national level. ✗

The **next three cases** relate to the national level. ✔

But numbers go before any other modifying word.

Additional three tests were carried out to discover why the machine kept cutting out. ✗

Three additional tests were carried out to discover why the machine kept cutting out. ✔

These are the **main two contributions** of this study. ✗

These are the **two main contributions** of this study. ✔

REVEALED: 16.3 *– How to use ordinal numbers effectively*

Ordinal numbers are used for order and rank. These numbers should not be used to represent a quantity.

Fourteenth sets of fermentations were performed using samples from . . . ✗

Fourteen sets of fermentations were performed using samples from . . . ✔

Here, an ordinal is required, but a cardinal number has been used by mistake.

A study reported it as the **eight** most common cause of _____ in the US. ✗

A study reported it as the **eighth** most common cause of _____ in the US. ✔

➤ RELATED ERRORS:

Writers should benefit from the following list, as these terms are generally misused and misspelled.

two	**2nd**	**second**	*2th*
four	**4th**	**fourth**	*forth*
eleven	**11th**	**eleventh**	*11st*
twelve	**12th**	**twelfth**	*twelvth*
seventeen	**17th**	**seventeenth**	*sevententh*
forty	**40th**	**fortieth**	*fourty* *fourtieth*

The forms 'fourth', and 'forty' are the most problematic. Remember that '4th' has a 'u' but '40' does not.

Fourty participants took part in the next stage. ✗

Forty *participants took part in the next stage.* ✔

It was the **forth** *time that the bill had been delayed.* ✗

It was the **fourth** *time that the bill had been delayed.* ✔

!   There is no need to use the word 'rank' here.

'Little opportunity for training' was **fourth rank** *on the list.* ✗
'Little opportunity for training' was **fourth** *on the list.* ✔

REVEALED: 16.4 – *The relationship between rank and article use*

A definite article is normally used when referring to a particular rank, because rank implies that only one thing can represent each place. This is demonstrated in the following example, where 'first' is used as an adjective.

The first *problem is whether there is enough memory to carry out all these tasks.*

But when used as an adverb that expresses the order of a list of points, no article is required.

*The first, we will look at the attitude of the workers; **the second**, their background and general work experience...* ✘

***First**, we will look at the attitude of the workers; **second**, their background and general work experience...* ✔

REVEALED: 16.5 *– How to use fractions correctly*

The main issues with fractions are failing to pluralize the term and using ordinal numbers.

*In other words, **two third** of the students felt that the amount of written English support was low.* ✘

*In other words, **two-thirds** of the students felt that the amount of written English support was low.* ✔

***Third quarters** of the respondents answered 'very often' for question 12.* ✘

***Three-quarters** of the respondents answered 'very often' for question 12.* ✔

▶ RELATED ERRORS:

twice/double

It is often difficult to choose between these related terms in a given situation. 'Twice' can only be used as an adverb; 'double' can be used as a noun, adjective, adverb, and verb. There is some overlap in meaning, but as a guideline 'twice' is used for 'two times' and for comparison alongside 'as'. 'Double' is used for expressing quantity, specifically for multiplying by two or as much again in size, strength, or number.

*In this scenario, the dose would be **twice**.* ✘
*In this scenario, the dose would be **doubled**.* ✔

*There were **double as** many withdrawals...* ✘
*There were **twice as** many withdrawals...* ✔

REVEALED: 16.6 – *Which prepositions to select for certain number-related phrases*

The following phrases are employed with numbers, but writers often select the wrong particle. A number can be divided 'by' another number, but not 'with', 'to', or 'into'. For the second error, there is a choice between 'equal to' and 'equals'.

divided by

> The number of components is then **divided into** the number of devices. ✘

> The number of components is then **divided by** the number of devices. ✔

equal to/equals

> They assert that the value of a leveraged firm is **equal with** the value of an unleveraged firm plus tax shield. ✘

> They assert that the value of a leveraged firm **equals to** the value of an unleveraged firm plus tax shield. ✘

> They assert that the value of a leveraged firm **is equal to** the value of an unleveraged firm plus tax shield. ✔   OR

> They assert that the value of a leveraged firm **equals** the value . . . ✔

REVEALED: 16.7 – *How to format percentages correctly in a sentence*

The percentage sign (%) is preferred to words when using percentages in the main text.

> The success rate was slightly lower than **60 percent**. ✘

> The success rate was slightly lower than **60%**. ✔

But if the sentence begins with a percentage, then the term should be written without numbers or signs.

> **70%** is acceptable in year one. ✘

> **Seventy percent** is acceptable in year one. ✔

If there are no numbers attached to the term, then the phrase to use is 'percentage' not 'percent'.

A small percent will be caused by poor visibility or low temperatures. ✘

A small percentage will be caused by poor visibility or low temperatures. ✔

These figures are also written in **percents**. ✘

These figures are also written in **percentages**. ✔

|➤ RELATED ERRORS:

When providing percentages in the results section, the 'of phrase' is likely to be needed, though it is usually left out in error.

Twenty percent teachers completed this task within the time allowed. ✘

Twenty percent of the teachers completed this task within the time allowed. ✔

But in the second school only *80% learners* achieved this. ✘

But in the second school only **80% of the learners** achieved this. ✔

When the percentage is acting like an adjective, then the 'of' phrase will not be required.

The machine had a **68% success rate** for this task.

* * *

For subject-verb agreement, the noun following the percentage should determine whether the verb is singular or plural. Here 'patients' is a plural noun, so a plural verb form ('are') is required.

As a result, 20% of the patients *is* eligible to proceed to the next phase. ✘

As a result, 20% of the patients **are** eligible to proceed to the next phase. ✔

In this next example an uncountable noun ('training') is used, so the verb has to be singular to agree.

According to the report, 25% of the training *were* supervised. ✘

According to the report, 25% of the training **was** supervised. ✔

The noun and not the percentage will also determine the verb form for these terms. Note that, in general, 'fewer' is used with countable nouns and 'less' with uncountable.

Less than 20% of the patients are eligible ... ✗
Fewer than 20% of the patients are eligible ... ✔

Fewer than 25% of the training was supervised. ✗
Less than 25% of the training was supervised. ✔

16.8 Exercises

A. Three sentences contain number errors, and three sentences are written correctly. Can you identify them?

The 19th section of the report lists the occasions when this can occur.

Brooks, C. 2014. *Introductory Econometrics for Finance*. 3rd ed. Cambridge: Cambridge University Press.

The forth reason is related to location, and the fifth reason is external investment.

19 out of 60 of the studies reviewed rejected the hypothesis put forward by Klinger (2002).

The company came seven in a list of the top ten companies in revenue.

Almost three-quarters of the respondents 'strongly agreed' with this statement.

B. Fill in each gap with an appropriate form.

percentage   percent   %

These are all written as a _____

Sixty-seven _____ were absent on the final day.

At least 60 _____ are in favour.

The _____ of people who then report this has decreased, though.

17
FIGURES AND TABLES

Focus on . . . Articles with figures and tables

Tense with figures and tables

This chapter focuses on the terms to use when referring to figures and tables. It covers the areas of article use, tense, prepositions, and verb choice.

17.1 numbered figures / 17.2 using 'above' and 'below' /
17.3 verb choice / 17.4 Exercises

Featured errors in 17:

above (17.2)	following (17.1)
according to (17.3)	in (17.1, 17.3)
as shown (17.3)	next (17.1, 17.3)
below (17.2)	on (17.1)
exhibit (17.3)	previous (17.1)

REVEALED: 17.1 – *How to refer to parts of an essay that are numbered*

When figures (diagrams and images) and tables are numbered, the noun takes on the properties of a proper noun. This means the definite article (*the*) is not needed.

> This can be seen **in the Figure 4** below. ✗
> This can be seen in **Figure 4** below. ✔

> Without the number, the noun will require a definite article.
>
> *This can be seen in **the** figure below.*

> As shown in **the Table 3**, this is not the case for SMEs. ✗
> As shown in **Table 3**, this is not the case for SMEs. ✔

When sequence words are used (next, previous, following, etc.), a number should not be added. These terms require an article and already indicate which figure is being referred to. The reference number can be written in brackets for clarification.

> In the **next Table 2.4**, the results from the second session are presented. ✗
> In the **next table**, the results from the second session are presented. ✔
> In the **next table (2.4)**, the results from the second session are presented. ✔

> 'In' should be used for tables and figures, not 'on'.
>
> **On** the following table, the studies relating to this topic are presented. ✗
> **In** the following table, the studies relating to this topic are presented. ✔
>
> (See also 7.1.)

> The **previous equation 3.4** is also useful for this task. ✗
> The **previous equation (3.4)** is also useful for this task. ✔
> **Equation 3.4** is also useful for this task. ✔

REVEALED: 17.2 – *How to refer to figures correctly when using 'above' and 'below'*

Readers are often guided to sections and figures that are below or above the text they are reading. The problem is that these two terms have different usages.

Both are used as prepositions. 'Below' is also an adverb, whereas 'above' can be an adverb or an adjective. This means that 'below' cannot come before a noun like this:

*This can be seen in the **below figure**.* ✗

*This can be seen in the **figure below**.* ✔

'Below' can be used before 'is/are'.

***Below** is a table displaying these results.*

'Above' is more flexible and can be used as an adjective before a noun.

*The **above** diagram does not address the issues at the lower level.*

But as an adverb it must come after the verb.

*As **above argued**, the importance of this will change depending on the makeup of the sample.* ✗

*As **argued above**, the importance of this will change depending on the makeup of the sample.* ✔

REVEALED: 17.3 – *Which verbs to use when introducing figures*

When referring to tables and figures, the following verbs are typical:

to show   to depict   to display   to see   to present

One error that should be addressed is the use of 'exhibit'.

*The breakdown of these results is **exhibited** in Table 4.* ✗

*The breakdown of these results is **shown/displayed** in Table 4.* ✔

The figure should not be labelled 'exhibit' either.

> *This has been provided in **Exhibit 3** below.* ✘

*   *   *

Naturally, the tense has to match the position of the table or figure and the terms employed.

> *This next model (3.5) **demonstrated** how key variables were selected.* ✘
> *This next model (3.5) **demonstrates** how key variables were selected.* ✔

If the figure is located close to the description, then the present tense is employed.

> *Figure 2.4 **shows** the model adapted from Lu (2013).*

> There is no need to use the past tense for introducing a figure located directly above the text.
>
> *Figure 2.4 (above) **showed** that this rate has dropped significantly in the past five years.* ✘
> *Figure 2.4 (above) **shows** that this rate has dropped significantly in the past five years.* ✔

▷ RELATED ERRORS:

Two phrases that are often used to refer to a figure or table are 'as shown' and 'according to'.

> ***As it is shown** in Table 2 . . .* ✘
> ***According to Table 2** it shows that the number of firms increased substantially in the 1990s.* ✘

Both of these have to be rewritten to simplify them and improve their clarity. The first has to be changed to:

> ***As shown** in Table 2 . . .* ✔

There are two options for the second phrase. Either

> *Table 2 shows*   or   *According to Table 2,*

There is no need to add a reporting verb ('shows') or to repeat the subject ('it') when the sentence begins with 'According to'.

> ***According to Table 2**, the number of firms increased substantially in the 1990s.* ✔

(See also 20.4.)

But care must be taken, because the phrase cannot always be used as a straight substitute for 'in'. 'According to' relates to the information within the figure, not just the figure in general.

> *'According to Figure 3' is a shortened version of 'According to the data/results in Figure 3'.*

It can also mean 'in agreement with'.

> *According to (the method/instruction/guidelines presented in) . . .*

It therefore sounds strange when used for just referring generally to the figure. In fact, often these introductory phrases are redundant and the reference to the figure can simply be placed within brackets.

> *We have taken each study and assessed its strengths and weaknesses **according to** Figure 7.* ✘
>
> *We have taken each study and assessed its strengths and weaknesses **(Figure 7)**.* ✔

17.4 Exercises

A. For the three sets of sentences that introduce a table, tick the option that is correct.

The Table 4 below shows the relationships among the four variables.

The below table 4 shows the relationships among the four variables.

Table 4 below shows the relationships among the four variables.

This is showed in Table 7 below.

This is shown in the below Table 7.

This is shown in Table 7 below.

According to the table below, the only support the scheme received was from Morgan (2006).

According to the table below, it shows that the only support the scheme received was from Morgan (2006).

According to table below, the only support the scheme received was from Morgan (2006).

B. Rewrite the following sentences to make them error-free.

The following Table 6.3 presents the findings of our study.

_____

This will be demonstrated in the Figures 3.1–3.4 above.

_____

Previous model 4.1 presents the four algorithms.

_____

Below diagram (Figure 7) outlines these provisions.

_____

18
SPELLING AND TYPOS

Focus on . . . Commonly misspelled words

Typos

This chapter presents spelling errors that are caused by confusing certain terms, picking up bad habits, and simply mistyping.

Background / 18.1 misspelled terms /
18.2 issues with double consonants / 18.3 Exercises

Featured errors in 18:

See list (18.1) plus . . .   identify (18.1)
assess (18.2)   occasion (18.2)
costumer (18.1)   occurrence (18.2)
diverse (18.1)   possess (18.2)

BACKGROUND: Certain spelling mistakes are merely the result of mistyping. Some occur because the writer has been influenced by similar-looking words or by a common order of letters, and others through mixing up vowels or because of the presence of double consonants. Recognition of the particular terms that are commonly misspelled will increase awareness and should lead to more care being taken to ensure they have been written correctly.

REVEALED: 18.1 – *Terms most often misspelled*

adjust/ajust

*These figures will then have to be **ajusted** to reflect the extra days.* ✘

*These figures will then have to be **adjusted** to reflect the extra days.* ✔

align/aline

*Their arguments **aline** with those of Patel and Guthrie (2009).* ✘

*Their arguments **align** with those of Patel and Guthrie (2009).* ✔

beginning/begging

*The advantage is that there is a clear **begging** and end that can be measured.* ✘

*The advantage is that there is a clear **beginning** and end that can be measured.* ✔

combining/combing

***Combing** these therapies has yielded impressive results.* ✘

***Combining** these therapies has yielded impressive results.* ✔

continuous/continues

*It focuses on developing these experiences and **continues** learning.* ✘

*It focuses on developing these experiences and **continuous** learning.* ✔

country/county

*The data were collected from six **counties** in the first stage.* ✘

*The data were collected from six **countries** in the first stage.* ✔

customer/costumer

*Yu (2015) analysed the relationship between the staff and the **costumers**.* ✘

*Yu (2015) analysed the relationship between the staff and the **customers**.* ✔

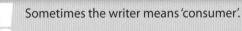

Sometimes the writer means 'consumer'.

*This comes under the topic of **costumer** rights.* ✘
*This comes under the topic of **consumer** rights.* ✔

even though/thought

*The proposal was submitted to the management, **even thought** the projections had yet to be made.* ✘

*The proposal was submitted to the management, **even though** the projections had yet to be made.* ✔

from/form

*These were obtained **form** a digital imaging company.* ✘
*These were obtained **from** a digital imaging company.* ✔

language/langauge

***Langauge** acquisition can be measured in a variety of ways.* ✘
***Language** acquisition can be measured in a variety of ways.* ✔

learning/leaning

*It was a great **leaning** experience for the tutors.* ✘
*It was a great **learning** experience for the tutors.* ✔

linear/liner

*The **liner** regression model is described below:* ✘
*The **linear** regression model is described below:* ✔

manager/manger

*Many of these studies interviewed workplace **mangers** about the effects it has on staff.* ✗

*Many of these studies interviewed workplace **managers** about the effects it has on staff.* ✔

phase/phrase

*This is likely to be a common occurrence in the design and development **phrases** of the project.* ✗

*This is likely to be a common occurrence in the design and development **phases** of the project.* ✔

previous/pervious

*This was primarily based on their **pervious** teaching experiences.* ✗

*This was primarily based on their **previous** teaching experiences.* ✔

severe/sever

*This has triggered **sever** competition between both the regions.* ✗

*This has triggered **severe** competition between both the regions.* ✔

A similar mistake occurs with diverse/divers.

*Conversely, there was a **divers** group in Morgan's (1999) study.* ✗

*Conversely, there was a **diverse** group in Morgan's (1999) study.* ✔

whether/weather

*Several studies have attempted to determine **weather** hedging is important in specific emerging markets.* ✗

*Several studies have attempted to determine **whether** hedging is important in specific emerging markets.* ✔

widely/wildly

> As the coordinates were **wildly** spread, the demonstrators were given 50 minutes to complete the route. ✘

> As the coordinates were **widely** spread, the demonstrators were given 50 minutes to complete the route. ✔

▶ RELATED ERRORS:

One of the most misspelled words in academic English is 'identify'. The spelling error even generates over half a million hits on Internet search engines.

> The second aim was to **indentify** models of community intervention employed by social workers. ✘

> The second aim was to **identify** models of community intervention employed by social workers. ✔

REVEALED: 18.2 – *How to spell certain terms that contain double consonants*

Good concentration can help to reduce spelling errors, but there are some terms that really can prove difficult to get right every time. Terms with sets of double letters need careful consideration.

> In order to **asess** the physical properties, a differential scale was used. ✘

> In order to **assess** the physical properties, a differential scale was used. ✔

> This species has been proven to **posses** the ability to discriminate between this polarized light. ✘

> This species has been proven to **possess** the ability to discriminate between this polarized light. ✔

The third person singular contains a further 's', making five in total.

Hardouvelis (1987) **assesses** *five different market indexes, including the S&P 500.*

It is also difficult to remember where to place the double letters for these terms.

*On this **occassion** the performance exceeded their expectations.* ✘
*On this **occasion** the performance exceeded their expectations.* ✔

*This is used to measure the **occurence** of unanticipated events.* ✘
*This is used to measure the **occurrence** of unanticipated events.* ✔

18.3 Exercises

A. There are ten spelling/typo mistakes in this passage. Can you find them all?

Every project must go though different phrases with different teams involved. This next section indentifies the phases in which the mangement team feature to from an overall picture of their role and influence. Perviously we looked at the design teams and how they alined their ideas with the production team. The aim is to create a product that the costumer identifies with. This is were feedback is also important, so the teams can lean about what the customer desires.

19
PUNCTUATION

Focus on . . . Punctuation (commas, semicolons, and dashes)
Capital letters

This chapter investigates the role certain punctuation marks play in writing. It focuses on comma placement, semicolon use, the three types of dash, and when to employ capital letters.

Background / 19.1 commas and clauses /
19.2 commas, conjunctions, and references /
19.3 semicolons, clauses, and lists / 19.4 distinguishing dashes /
19.5 capital letter use / 19.6 Exercises

Featured errors in 19:

although (19.1)	unless (19.2)
but (19.2)	well (19.4)
however (19.3, 19.5)	whereas (19.2)
if (19.1)	

BACKGROUND: Punctuation is used to organize writing, enhance readability, and promote understanding. Too much punctuation or too little will make for an unpleasant reading experience; the wrong punctuation will obscure or even change the meaning of a sentence. The position of a comma, or its absence, can markedly alter the context.

> *For the first task, the participants could choose among a magnetic compass or a GPS compass, a mobile phone with GPS enabled, our experimental device with instructions or a map.*

> *For the first task, the participants could choose among a magnetic compass or a GPS compass, a mobile phone with GPS enabled, our experimental device with instructions, or a map.*

In the first example, it may appear to some that a participant can choose the experimental device and then decide whether to have instructions with it or have a map. In the second example, with the addition of a comma, the options seem to be a device OR a map.

In some cases, the sentence is unreadable if the comma is in the wrong place.

> *If it is not carried out the opportunity to provide students with feedback, will be missed.* ✗

> **If it is not carried out,** *the opportunity to provide students with feedback will be missed.* ✔

See 20.5 for information on the three-point ellipsis.

REVEALED: 19.1 – *The relationship between commas and clauses*

Commas should not be used to split up sentences that are independent and represent two different thoughts. Full stops (periods) should be used for this.

> *To answer this, we looked at artists that had used this technique in their work, we discovered that a number of painters relied heavily on red, black, and white.* ✗

> *To answer this, we looked at artists that had used this technique in their work. We discovered that a number of painters relied heavily on red, black, and white.* ✔

*   *   *

A dependent clause can appear within another clause in a sentence to give additional (but not essential) information (see 10B). Commas are placed on each side of the dependent clause.

The export data of the countries were analysed, **with the exception of Thailand,** *and then tabulated according to their region (Tables 3.4–3.9).*

But in this next sentence the middle clause is not additional information. It should be the start of a new sentence because it does not follow on from the opening independent clause. This method of splitting up every part with a comma is a common mistake.

Ten variables were selected for this study, **to avoid the temptation of including as many variables as possible,** *only items with missing variables were used.* ✘

Ten variables were selected for this study. **To avoid the temptation of including as many variables as possible, only items with missing variables were used.** ✔

When a sentence begins with a dependent clause, a comma is used to separate it from the independent clause.

If the device is in this mode for longer than six hours, *then the batteries will need to be replaced.*

A comma is not required if an independent clause comes first, unless a connecting word that relates to contrast or concession (unless, although, whereas . . .) begins the dependent clause.

The participants are allowed to converse, if the instructions have already been given. ✘

The participants are allowed to converse if the instructions have already been given. ✔

Hseih and Fu (2003) increased this number to ten although they searched within a smaller area. ✘

Hseih and Fu (2003) increased this number to ten, although they searched within a smaller area. ✔

REVEALED: 19.2 – *Where to place commas when using conjunctions*

Commas should always be placed before a connecting word, not after.

> *These researchers noted the difficulties that they encountered when reaching their target participants* **whereas,** *Hu (1988) used the learners from the institution.* ✘

> *These researchers noted the difficulties that they encountered when reaching their target participants***,** **whereas** *Hu (1988) used the learners from the institution.* ✔

> *The conditions cannot be changed at a later date* **unless,** *a factual error has been made in the document.* ✘

> *The conditions cannot be changed at a later date***,** **unless** *a factual error has been made in the document.* ✔

> *The government subsequently introduced free primary education* **but,** *this was not accompanied by the necessary financial support.* ✘

> *The government subsequently introduced free primary education***,** **but** *this was not accompanied by the necessary financial support.* ✔

REVEALED: 19.3 – *When to use a semicolon in a clause and in a list*

Semicolons are more powerful than commas and can be employed when two clauses are being contrasted.

> *The first method produced sufficient simulation time and was able to determine unique values**;** the second method failed in both these tasks.*

When a conjunctive adverb is used to break up two independent clauses, a semicolon is placed before this connecting word and a comma after it.

> *The third group scored higher than the other two groups on all of the tasks**;*** **however***, their accuracy was the lowest for half of the tasks carried out.*

When additional information is being provided for each entry in a list, commas and semicolons should be used together to break up entries and improve readability. The writer here is using lists within a list and the semicolons serve to divide the entries clearly.

*It included questions about **demographics**, such as socioeconomic status and household structure**; life events**, including early life exposure**; healthy and unhealthy habits,** such as smoking, alcohol intake, and drug use**; general health**, including reproductive events and illnesses;* ... ✔

Without the semicolons, the list would be more difficult to interpret and the main categories (in bold above) would not be easily recognized. In this next example it is hard to tell whether these elements all come under the heading of demographics or are separate categories.

It included questions about demographics, such as socioeconomic status and household structure, life events, including early life exposure, healthy and unhealthy habits, such as smoking ... ✗

REVEALED: 19.4 – *The different types of dash and how they are employed*

There are three types of dash.

hyphen -

en dash –

em dash —

Hyphens are the smallest of the three horizontal lines. They connect words and word fragments. They are commonly found in compounds that are modifying a noun and coming before the noun.

*This is a **well defined** concept, but little has been written about its application in the field.* ✗

*This is a **well-defined** concept, but little has been written about its application in the field.* ✔

> ❗ But when the term comes after the noun, a hyphen is not required.
>
> *The different stages of this process have been **well defined**.* (See also 8.1.)

The en dash is the length of a standard 'n' and is used mainly for notation to repre-sent ranges and to split up names and opposites.

*. . . as seen in Robertson and Davies (1998, pp. **110–118**)*

*The **2011–2012** report was also made available online for six months.*

The em dash is slightly longer than the en dash and has two functions. It is used at the end of a sentence for a final thought or a restatement of a previous thought. It is especially useful in long sentences when a set of commas has already been used. Only one dash is used for this task.

The data are available to all staff, especially data related to the outcomes of relevant trials, but training is required on effective search techniques—as observed in our study.

It can also be used in pairs instead of commas or brackets to add emphasis and to clarify, or if the phrase interrupts the previous one. Brackets should be used for information that carries little real importance.

*If the infant has reached a suitable weight **usually around 5 kg** then dialysis would also be an option.* ✗

*If the infant has reached a suitable weight—**usually around 5 kg**—then dialysis would also be an option.* ✔

Two hyphens cannot represent an em dash.

. . . as many of the political parties focused on this issue of nationalism--an idea originally put forward by a respected commentator prior to the campaigns. ✗

. . . as many of the political parties focused on this issue of nationalism—an idea originally put forward by a respected commentator prior to the campaigns. ✔

REVEALED: 19.5 *– When to use capital letters*

Many writers use capital letters in a seemingly random manner. Only proper nouns such as names of places (see also 14.B and 14.2), companies, organizations, titles, people, days, and months should really be given capitals—this includes adjectives derived from people's names and places.

Dr Wenja Wang	Chinese	the Red Cross	Shakespearian
Shandong University	Microsoft	He Luting	June

The following example demonstrates the casual use of capital letters that some writers adopt:

> This **Study** is going to build a new model based on the previous studies about **Consumer Value**, motivation, and expectation to explore the differences. Initially, **Quantitative** methods will be used to collect **First-hand** data in the **uk** and in **china**. ✗

This should be rewritten so only the two countries have capital letters.

> This study is going to build a new model based on the previous studies about consumer value, motivation, and expectation to explore the differences. Initially, quantitative methods will be used to collect first-hand data in the **UK** and in **China**. ✔

Capital letters should come after full stops and question marks but not after commas or semicolons. These next examples are typical mistakes that demonstrate this point.

> How can the company change the mentality of the employees? **we** will try to answer this question by first analysing why … ✗

> How can the company change the mentality of the employees? **We** will try to answer this question by first analysing why … ✔

> Similarly, **The** two Chinese companies also tried to attract foreign investment. ✗

> Similarly, **the** two Chinese companies also tried to attract foreign investment. ✔

> It was clear that most of the respondents had at least some exposure to this; **However**, the distribution was slightly skewed to the left. ✗

> It was clear that most of the respondents had at least some exposure to this; **however**, the distribution was slightly skewed to the left. ✔

*   *   *

It is important to have a consistent format in the contents page of a paper. Often the main chapter headings are capitalized and the subheadings lower case, but some subject guidelines suggest all titles should have initial capitals for each word. The following is a good example of inconsistent capital letter use.

A more consistent format would be to capitalize the initial letter of all the words (apart from prepositions and articles) except those in the subsections (2.3.1 and 2.3.2).

19.6 Exercises

A. Insert appropriate punctuation into these passages.

The dissertation is divided into five chapters in this chapter I introduced the rationale and the aims of this study from which the research questions were drawn

The final objective is to understand learners perceptions of the text which ties in with objective three

The authors would like to thank mr Michael morgan for his feedback on the model we would also like to thank orion solutions for lending us the equipment to carry out the experiments the first experiment used their original RH200 system the second experiment required the upgrade

The uk and china are two other countries that have well established trading relationships Huang 2010 pp 23 45

The leverage is positively related to these tax shields in the real estate industry although the outcome is not statistically significant

The participants are studying subjects at the Arts School primarily Graphics and Illustration in the south of the district

B. Circle the capital letters that are not required.

When we were informed that there would only be four people in the Focus Group, we were not expecting the group to be that informative. According to Chen (1998), from his book *Research Methods in Action*, such a small group was unlikely to generate the Group Dynamics necessary for an outstanding session; However, the focus group actually turned out to be very informative, and all the questions we prepared for the Discussion were fully answered with interesting insights from the Participants.

20

REFERENCING

Focus on . . . In-text citing

Reporting verbs

Quotes

This chapter reveals the typical errors made when referencing other people's work in the main text and in the bibliography. The topics covered include formatting, names of authors, subject-verb problems, and handling quotes.

Background / 20.1 Harvard and APA styles / 20.2 names / 20.3 verb agreement / 20.4 phrases and reporting verbs / 20.5 using quotes / 20.6 Exercises

Featured errors in 20:

according to (20.4)   et al. (20.3)
by (20.4)   of (20.4)
concern (20.4)   say (20.4)

BACKGROUND: There are two types of reference in a piece of research: an in-text reference (usually containing an author and a year) that is placed in the text, and a full reference (including also the title and publisher's details) that forms part of a list located at the end of a paper. It is important to understand that even if a researcher is not being directly quoted, the study has to be referenced if the ideas or evidence are being used. In this first example, the author has been paraphrased but still has to be cited because the writer could not have known this information before consulting the book.

> *The original objective of this policy was to improve the quality of education in schools located in the north of the country (Lu 2012).*

Unless it is a well-known fact or an obvious statement, an author's work has to be cited.

In the reference list at the end (also called a bibliography), all of the works that have been referred to in the paper have to be listed (usually alphabetically, unless the number system is being used). A separate list headed 'works consulted' can be created for books and articles that served as background reading but were not utilized in the paper.

REVEALED: 20.1 – *How to format in-text references in Harvard and APA styles*

There are a number of different formats for referencing in-text. Writers following the name system used by both Harvard and APA should take note of the following:

When directly mentioning an author's study in the text, there should only be brackets around the date.

> *Managers could also delegate, as suggested by (Lu 2003).* ✘
> *Managers could also delegate, as suggested by **Lu (2003)**.* ✔

> *This was later modified by (Tan et al. 2000) to include impacts.* ✘
> *This was later modified by **Tan et al. (2000)** to include impacts.* ✔

The year must come directly after the author's name.

> *Ross claims that this measure may well cause controversy (2000).* ✘
> ***Ross (2000)** claims that this measure may well cause controversy.* ✔

Brackets should be placed around the author's name and date when the author's views are being expressed but the author is not being mentioned directly—and the citation should be at the end of the sentence or quote.

> *Therefore, these values should not be regarded as absolute quantities **(Tan et al. 2000)**.*

If the author has not been mentioned directly, then they cannot be directly referred to in the next sentence.

> *Individual difference is another factor that will need to be considered (Madsen et al., 2005). **They** maintain that out of the five . . .* ✘
>
> ***Madsen et al. (2005)** believe that individual difference is another factor that should be considered. **They** maintain that out of the five . . .* ✔

*   *   *

In Harvard style, page numbers are normally used for all in-text references, unless an author is just referring generally to another study:

> *Hu (2001: 22) views Hunt's (1999) work as crucial.*

APA requires page numbers only for direct quotes.

> HARVARD: *Yokohama is a unique urban centre with elevated highways and sky-scrapers but also a traditional and well-preserved centre (Kondo 2006: 25).*
>
> APA: *Yokohama is a unique urban centre with elevated highways and skyscrapers but also a traditional and well-preserved centre (Kondo, 2006).*

The only other key difference between Harvard and APA is that the year is put in brackets in the reference list in APA. Most Harvard versions omit the brackets.

> Harvard: Leung, H. 2015. *Reinventing maths*. Oxford: Oxford University Press.
>
> APA: Leung, H. (2015). *Reinventing maths*. Oxford: Oxford University Press.

REVEALED: 20.2 – *How to use names correctly when referencing*

When a researcher or research is being cited, it is important to use the researcher's family name or surname. Often writers use the given (first) name by mistake.

<table>
<tr><td style="text-align:center">Michael</td><td style="text-align:center">Morgan</td></tr>
<tr><td style="text-align:center">(first name/given name)</td><td style="text-align:center">(family name/surname)</td></tr>
</table>

> ***Michael*** *(2009) addresses this by looking at the influence these companies have over the government-led committees.* ✗

> ***Morgan*** *(2009) addresses this by looking at the influence these companies have over the government-led committees.* ✔

The surname will be written first in the reference list, but it will have a comma after it to indicate that it is the surname and not the first name.

Morgan, M. 2014. Defining blood stem cells, *Stem Cell Research* **4**, 15–23.

REVEALED: 20.3 – *Which verb form to choose when referencing*

Subject-verb agreement (see 4) is a key ingredient of written English and can become quite complex. An easily recognizable but frequent mistake occurs when authors are being referred to.

In the following example, more than one author is being referred to so the verb must have a plural form (one study with two authors is also considered plural).

> *Smith et al.* **states** *that this is true for bull markets.* ✗

> *Smith et al.* **state** *that this is true for bull markets.* ✔

> **!**
> The correct form for multiple authors is et al.
>
> The following are typical errors:
>
> *Smith at al.   Smith et all.   Smith etal.*   (See also 9.3.)

> *Morgan and Jones (2003)* ***proposes*** *focusing on the consumer.* ✗

> *Morgan and Jones (2003)* ***propose*** *focusing on the consumer.* ✔

In this next example, the study is the subject rather than the authors so the verb is singular.

*A study by Cheung and Park (2009) **have** located this weak point in the structure.* ✘

*A study by Cheung and Park (2009) **has** located this weak point in the structure.* ✔

And here, more than one study is being referred to so the plural applies again.

*Smith (2003) and Morgan (2010) also **considers** why this might affect efficiency.* ✘

*Smith (2003) and Morgan (2010) also **consider** why this might affect efficiency.* ✔

REVEALED: 20.4 – *Which terms to use when referencing a study*

When introducing a researcher and a study, there are certain phrases and reporting words that can be employed. The writer has used the wrong preposition in the first example; in the second example, the subject has been needlessly repeated and a verb unnecessarily added.

*A study **of** Morgan (1998) tested the effectiveness of the algorithm.* ✘

*A study **by** Morgan (1998) tested the effectiveness of the algorithm.* ✔

*According to Cho (1989) **he believes** the situation will only improve if investment is found from external sources.* ✘

According to Cho (1989), the situation will only improve if investment is found from external sources. ✔   (See also 17.3.)

Reporting verbs have specific meanings and therefore are prone to being used incorrectly. When an author has a strong opinion, instead of employing a weak verb such as 'says' the writer can use 'asserts' / 'declares' / 'maintains' . . .

*Kim (2010) **says** that this had actually occurred the year before.* ✘

*Kim (2010) **asserts** that this had actually occurred the year before.* ✔

Here are some other reporting verbs and their meanings.

When the author of the resource gives **guidance** or an **opinion**:

Kim (2010) proposes/recommends/predicts/projects/suggests . . .

When the author **looks closely** at something,

Kim (2010) analyses/focuses/theorizes . . .

When the author **uncovers** something:

Kim (2010) discovers/finds/learns/reveals . . .

When the author **does not believe in** something:

Kim (2010) denies/questions/refutes/rejects . . .

(See also 5.7.)

▶ RELATED ERRORS:

Forms of the verb 'to concern' should be avoided when introducing a researcher's work or study. The verb is often used in the wrong way.

*In his work, Leung (2003; 2005) **is concerned with** the inspiration behind the designs of Commes des Garçons.* ✘

*In his work, Leung (2003; 2005) **looks at/considers** the inspiration behind the designs of Commes des Garçons.* ✔

*Suto (2010) **concerns about** the artist's technique in these three pieces and concludes that . . .* ✘

*Suto (2010) **considers/assesses** the artist's technique in these three pieces and concludes that . . .* ✔

(See also 12.1.)

REVEALED: 20.5 – *How to use quotes effectively in essays*

The main issues with quotes are failing to copy the quote correctly (which can be easily avoided with better concentration), failing to close the quote with a quotation mark, and failing to match the end of the introduction to the beginning of the quote. In this first example, the quotation has not been closed.

*Sandelowski (2000: 34) described this as '**all inquiry entails description, and all description entails interpretation**. Another aspect of this is . . .* ✘

*Sandelowski (2000: 34) described this as '**all inquiry entails description, and all description entails interpretation**'. Another aspect of this is . . .* ✔

A common error is failing to match the beginning of the quote with the sentence that introduces it. The writer has not achieved a smooth and continuous transition in either of these examples.

> *Structural change can be **defined as** 'it is the different arrangements of productive activity in the economy . . .* ✘
>
> *Structural change can be **defined as 'the** different arrangements of productive activity in the economy . . .* ✔
>
> *As pointed out by Monroe (2009), '**the extent to which** countries differ in their degree of investor protection.'* ✘
>
> *As pointed out by Monroe (2009), **the rules determine '**the extent to which** countries differ in their degree of investor protection.'* ✔

*   *   *

Lengthy quotes can be reduced by using the three-point ellipsis so only the important points are presented. The first extract is the quote in full; in the second extract, an ellipsis has been employed to make the quote shorter and more relevant to the writer's main argument or point.

> 1. 'It is clear that the government is intent on directing polytechnics to develop along the lines it prefers. It is hard to fault this approach, but there is an inevitable conflict created between the expectations and needs of the communities which the Polytechnic serves—as expressed in its charter, mission statement and strategic plan objectives—and the directions of central government. It would, in my view, be more honest if the government was to state unequivocally that we are an agency of government and, as such, expected to follow its directions. The present situation leaves the Polytechnic to defend itself against accusations that it is not meeting its charter obligations, whilst enabling the government to deny any responsibility.'

> 2. 'It is clear that the government is intent on directing polytechnics to develop along the lines it prefers . . . It would, in my view, be more honest if the government was to state unequivocally that we are an agency of government and, as such, expected to follow its directions. The present situation leaves the Polytechnic to defend itself against accusations that it is not meeting its charter obligations, whilst enabling the government to deny any responsibility.'

This three-point ellipsis can also be employed to ensure that the quote matches its introduction (see point above).

> *Kimberly (1986) stated that: '. . . the situation will only worsen for these marginal groups'.*

20.6 Exercises

A. Introduce these studies as concisely as possible and select an appropriate reporting verb using the notes provided. The first one has been done for you.

Morgan and two other researchers   year 1998   looking at housing market mainly UK

Morgan et al. (1998) focus on the UK housing market.
_____

Cho 2006 on page 61 disagrees with Tan's study from 1998 about enterprise zones

_____

_____

michael smith and colleagues wonder whether feedback is of good enough quality for students in universities in the UK. Research from 2014.

_____

_____

B. This quote needs to be reduced to about 20–25 words. Use three-point ellipses to achieve this, ensuring that clarity is also maintained.

Johnson et al. (2007) reviewed 19 definitions of mixed-methods and concluded that '*mixed-methods research is the type of research in which a researcher or team of researchers combines elements of qualitative and quantitative research approaches (e.g., use of qualitative and quantitative viewpoints, data collection, analysis, inference techniques) for the purposes of breadth and depth of understanding and corroboration. Mixed methods research provides the opportunity for triangulation, where the phenomenon under study can be assessed using various techniques and methods, and helps to develop a more complete understanding of the topic (p. 123).*'

_____

_____

_____

APPENDIX: Irregular Verbs

The past participle is used for the perfect tense (with 'to have'), in passive sentences (with 'to be') and as an adjective (before nouns and after linking verbs).

*This has **changed** in the past few years . . .*

*This section was **expanded** so both programs could be included.*

*The **expanded** section has allowed the programmers to . . .*

*This appears **reduced** when the surface becomes moist.*

For a regular verb, the past participle has the same form and spelling as the simple (normal) past tense and that ending is always the same (*–ed*). For irregular verbs, the endings can take on unusual forms. Here is an example.

Regular verb (smoke):   He smoked   He has **smoked**

Irregular verb (fall):   He fell   He has **fallen**

The first form is the past tense (*smoked, fell*). The second is the past participle (*smoked, fallen*). Note how the irregular verb's past participle has a different form from the past simple form (some do have the same form). Many of these irregular forms have no real pattern and must simply be learnt. For this reason, a list of key irregular verbs in both forms is presented below (see also 5.6):

Verb	Past tense	Past participle
to arise	arose	arisen
to awake	awoke	awoken
to be	was / were	been
to bear	bore	borne
to beat	beat	beaten
to become	became	become
to begin	began	begun
to bid	bid	bid
to break	broke	broken
to bring	brought	brought
to build	built	built
to buy	bought	bought
to catch	caught	caught
to choose	chose	chosen
to come	came	come
to deal	dealt	dealt
to do	did	done
to draw	drew	drawn
to drive	drove	driven
to eat	ate	eaten
to fall	fell	fallen
to find	found	found
to forbid	forbade	forbidden
to forget	forgot	forgot or forgotten
to forgive	forgave	forgiven
to freeze	froze	frozen
to get	got	got or gotten
to go	went	gone
to grow	grew	grown
to hide	hid	hidden
to know	knew	known
to lay	laid	laid
to lie (rest)	lay	lain
to prove	proved	proven
to ride	rode	ridden
to ring	rang	rung
to rise	rose	risen

Verb	Past tense	Past participle
to run	ran	run
to see	saw	seen
to show	showed	shown
to speak	spoke	spoken
to steal	stole	stolen
to strive	strove	striven
to take	took	taken
to wear	wore	worn
to write	wrote	written

ANSWERS

Answers to Chapter 1 (1.6)

A. The issues related to ~~healths~~ (**health**) and safety are discussed in the next section along with any ~~informations~~ (**information**) from the respondents of the employee survey. The training schedule and ~~transports advices~~ (**transport advice**) for field trips are attached to the Appendices to provide more details, to avoid any confusion. The ~~believes~~ (**beliefs**) of the employees will be assessed, with a focus on whether they actually ~~belief~~ (**believe**) in the new policy.

The economic development of this region of China has aroused the interest of research-ers of late. By means of SWOT analysis (which stands for ~~strengthens~~ (**strengths**), ~~weakness~~ (**weaknesses**), opportunities, and threats) I will assess the potential of the five SMEs from the area, with a focus on competition between the five regarding their capabilities. Any phenomena extracted from this analysis will form the basis for the second part of the study. Any experiences detailed by the business managers will also join those ~~phenom-enon~~ (**phenomena**) as evidence to inform policy.

B. Two (behaviour and development)

C. Countable:
Associating certain identities with certain behaviours can prove problematic.

Uncountable:
The two factors we will concentrate on are behaviour and change.

Countable:
They witnessed a number of new developments during this period.

Uncountable:
Personal development has been given plenty of attention by policymakers within higher education.

Answers to Chapter 2 (2.7)

A. It was important to contact employees from [an] SME in the region to see whether [the] theory was correct that these workers were not getting the training opportunities that the workers of larger corporations enjoyed. Contact was made first of all by [zero] email, and then three visits were made to [the] chosen company to conduct [zero] formal interviews.

B. Most previous investigations have been based on non-Chinese students lacking Chinese cultural values. Chinese learners have been greatly influenced by mainstream Chinese culture in their perception and behaviour when participating in ~~the~~ communication inside and outside **the** classroom. 'The Chinese learner' is characterized as being reticent in ~~the~~ class. Wen and Clément (2003) explain that ~~a~~ Chinese students are influenced by classic Confucianism, in particular examination-oriented learning, shaping their understanding and way of ~~the~~ learning.

C. Student attendance has dropped to 78% in the past three months at the college.

In case of an attack from another network user, three recommendations are given.

The quality of the products was also much higher.

It is possible that **the** author overlooked this peripheral region.

Answers to Chapter 3 (3.7)

A. A manager must ensure that he listens to his staff at all times.
A manager must ensure that they listen to the staff at all times.

Other issue is that the software took too long to load.
Another issue is that the software took too long to load.

There have been few problems with attendance, so they decided to warn the pupils.
There have been a few problems with attendance, so they decided to warn the pupils.

We can then change this into another formats.
We can then change this into another format. / We can then change this into other formats.

B. Both/All of the models failed to produce satisfactory results, so we decided to create our own.

(The fact that the author had to create their own model implies that none of the models was satisfactory, so the answer is unlikely to be 'one of the models' or 'some of the models'.)

It is important to make sure that with each draft **fewer** mistakes are made.

All/Some of the evidence points to the fact that these policies have failed to boost the economy. *('All' is more likely.)*

There is **less** risk involved, so these investors might be tempted.

(If the investors are risk-takers then 'some risk' is possible.)

This only worked for **one/some** of the regions, as revealed in Table 4.

There was **one** participant without knowledge of the procedure.

Answers to Chapter 4 (4.5)

A. The assistance provided to these people $\boxed{\text{is}}$ important because it is the only support available to them.

Networking in groups $\boxed{\text{is}}$ more effective than walking around as an individual is.

Educating these groups $\boxed{\text{prevents}}$ them from getting involved in crime and anti-social behaviour.

Workers who had enrolled in the scheme $\boxed{\text{were}}$ more likely to have a positive attitude towards their company.

Most of the students' perceived speaking improvements $\boxed{\text{are}}$ related to presentation skills.

B. We will also ask whether they have noticed an improvement in the past six months.

They can change this at any point during the process.

The teacher must decide if this is acceptable behaviour.

How can this system be changed to suit every department?

How these reports are assessed is another talking point.

What relationships can be formed when these two areas combine?

Answers to Chapter 5 (5.9)

A. There seems to be an issue with $\boxed{\text{extracting}}$ all the data from this program.
–ing form must follow a preposition ('with').

They should let the students $\boxed{\text{think}}$ for themselves some of the time.
The verb 'let' is followed by a verb in the base form (no 'to').

They were allowed $\boxed{\text{to change}}$ their minds and select a different object if they were not happy.
The verb 'allow' is used with a verb in the infinitive form (to + verb) in this construction.

Despite this $\boxed{\text{increasing}}$ the budget, the project was too expensive to carry out.
–ing form must follow a preposition ('despite').

B. Although three participants ~~withdraw~~ (**withdrew**) from the research, we had enough to ~~beginning~~ (**begin**) the experiment. Group A were all meant to ~~underwent~~ (**undergo**) the full experiment, but time constraints meant that they had to ~~chose~~ (**choose**) between the partial and the full experiment. Whenever the liquid ~~become~~ (**became**) too cloudy, the researcher asked an assistant to ~~shaken~~ (**shake**) the bottle, and when this happened the clock was stopped. SIX

C. *The following diagram demonstrates these connections and labels the stages.*

We designed the logo and then presented the final product.

This allowed them to change the final design and submit their work on time.

D. *The product was tested the following week.*

The class was asked to quieten down on a number of occasions.

The number of participants was reduced for the next stage.

Answers to Chapter 6 (6.5)

A. The next section would provide an evaluation of the three strategies. ✗
The next section will provide an evaluation of the three strategies.

We will also look at how they can improve their image? ✗
We will also look at how they can improve their image.

Different teachers should sets different projects to ensure there is variety. ✗
Different teachers should set different projects to ensure there is variety.

How does this affect their relationship with the staff? CORRECT

It could be essential for all students to register their interest beforehand. ✗
It is essential for all students to register their interest beforehand.

The reports does not include South America or Africa. ✗
The reports do not include South America or Africa.

B. The results **will/should** be available the following day if everything goes to plan.

Can they reduce their spending while retaining the quality of their product?

Tan (2003) rejected the claim that they **could** enter both markets successfully.

This **will** be discussed in the following chapter.

I **could** have selected managers but decided that the opinions of ordinary workers **would** be more useful.

Answers to Chapter 7 (7.5)

A. A discussion of these theories will take place **in** chapter seven.

Prior **to** becoming CEO, she worked in the public sector.

Only pupils that had a good disciplinary record could participate **in** the scheme.

Each participant was then assigned **to** one of five groups.

This could result **in** confusion, as the two departments would be dealing with the same cases.

Hopefully, this will address the needs **of** the marginalized groups.

In most cases this leads **to** prosecution, so it is more than worthwhile.

B.

result in   caused by   rely on

likelihood of   benefit from   combine with

Answers to Chapter 8 (8.8)

A. As Table 5 shows, the ⌐highest⌐ amount was recorded in Q2.

Less than 2% lost their jobs ⌐compared with⌐ 4% the year before.

These figures were ⌐lower⌐ than expected, considering many of their competitors had improved their positions.

These findings reveal 'InterTrain' to be the ⌐strongest⌐ brand of the five companies.

It has proven to be the ⌐least⌐ effective with the ⌐lowest⌐ scores across all four tests.

B. Given the current **global** competitiveness in this industry, if companies can find a way to conduct business effectively it will give them a **clear** advantage over their rivals. **Similarly,** if negotiations can be carried out efficiently and promptly, then more time can be devoted to research and development (R&D)—the focus of this paper. A **highly** regarded study on

R&D is Sheridan and Lo (2013), who looked at the **frequent** failure of three firms attempting to enhance their R&D output.

Answers to Chapter 9 (9.4)

A. This could prove difficult for **countries** not signing up to this scheme.

I will focus on five Asian **countries** for answering question five.

I will also look at this **country's** attitude towards consumer rights.

Most **countries'** policies differ in this respect, so it will require a deep analysis.

B. A distinction should be made between this cohort and the **native population**.

The session was **four hours** long and covered the key topics.

A **three-step** framework is now proposed that seeks to resolve this issue.

This particular **manager's viewpoint** is captured through a questionnaire and an interview.

Answers to Chapter 10 (10.8)

A. The collaboration was fairly successful. INDEPENDENT

Since my colleagues were unwilling to change the topic DEPENDENT

I made a suggestion about allocating tasks. INDEPENDENT

Although there were times when the group fell silent DEPENDENT

Without a coordinator in place during the meeting DEPENDENT

B. Naturally, the greater the dose, the faster the medication will work.

Not only should the tutor get involved but also a member of the senior management.

It is clear there is a component that has not been fitted properly.

C. These employees worked in the department **that** was going to be restructured.

They knew ~~that~~ this was only a temporary measure.

The roles ~~that~~ they filled were quite varied.

The students were relieved ~~that~~ the exams were finally over.

Answers to Chapter 11 (11.4)

A. There was no real difference between the two schemes.

Luo (1997) only looked at the figures that were important to the shareholders.

The presence of the senior management team seemed to affect the performance of the sales team on this task.

In positivist research, the researcher is interested in gaining knowledge.

B. Six

> When the degradation in the value of silver is combined with the diminution of the quantity of it contained in the coin of the same denomination, the ~~lose~~ (**loss**) is frequently still greater.

It was Adam Smith's ~~believe~~ (**belief**) that striving for personal gain is a natural human trait. Smith also ~~proofed~~ (**proved**) a number of other theories of the time, and the ~~extend~~ (**extent**) of his influence is still apparent today. Given its ~~economy~~ (**economic**) relevance, the ~~argue~~ (**argument**) put forward about the 'invisible hand' should be explored in more detail, and therefore a discussion will take place in the chapter that follows.

C. The aim was to interview at least three **men/women** and two **women/men** from each department.

One **male/female** rat was withdrawn from the process on account of its size.

Male/Female deaths were much lower for period four.

The number of **women/men** improving remained stable.

Women/Men are more likely to seek treatment early.

Answers to Chapter 12 (12.3)

A. *This will be explained in the **following** parts:*

*The advantages are described **as follows**:*

*The three recommendations **follow** a brief analysis.*

*An estimation of the cost will also **follow**.*

*The **following** are some suggestions:*

B. This will also ⌐raise¬ the price of the commodity in the short term.

The ⌐same¬ finding was reported by Chen (2009) and Tran (2013).

Some of the teachers ⌐considered¬ this measure and then agreed it could provide a solution to the problem.

The accuracy and the relevance of the content cannot be guaranteed, and this ⌐also¬ applies to any links that are provided on their pages.

C. dehydrate   dissimilar   inconsistent   nonspecific   reassess   uncomfortable

Answers to Chapter 13 (13.7)

A. Returning ~~back~~ to the original design, it is ~~very~~ obvious that the ~~brand~~ new model created by Smith Motors is ~~definitely~~ the best. We then ranked the companies in the order Orion, Dubaki, Renton Spares. Last ~~but not least~~ is Spades, but they were hampered by ~~crazy~~ misfortune when their mechanic was taken ill; their design team was also comparatively small ~~in number~~. This proved to be ~~very~~ critical, as Wu (2007) suggests that five members is optimal.

Based on the results ~~that have been stated~~ above, we conclude that . . .

B. ~~majorly~~ largely/greatly   ~~wildly~~ widely   ~~reckon~~   imagine/consider/suppose

~~couldn't~~ could not   ~~at last~~ last/finally   ~~basically~~   essentially/ultimately

Answers to Chapter 14 (14.4)

A. We interviewed three German employees, two Korean employees, and the manager of the company (who was born in Germany) at the Japanese headquarters in Tokyo.

A number of Chinese firms have been studied, two from the north of China and three from the south. We also discuss the findings of Yoshinaga (2009), who looked at the performance of Japanese firms listed on Japan's stock exchange.

B. Four

They identified how the ~~China~~ government can resolve this issue. (**Chinese**)

We focus on the UK, the US, Germany, and France. CORRECT

~~China~~ economy is beginning to emerge from the crisis. (**China's/The Chinese**)

~~France~~ steel companies have not suffered the same fate as their counterparts in the UK. (**French**)

We looked at the structure of the following languages: ~~Korea~~, Japanese, ~~Germany~~, English, and French. (**Korean . . . German**)

Answers to Chapter 15 (15.7)

A. Five

~~Since~~ (**From**) 2020 the headquarters will be in Munich. This move has come about because of ~~nowaday's~~ (**today's**) market, where production is centring on Germany. ~~On~~ (**In**) June the company issued a statement detailing the move and that within three years they wanted to streamline the business prior to relocation ~~on~~ (**in**) 2020. In recent years profits ~~were~~ (**have been**) declining, so action needed to be taken.

B. The government has been discussing this **since** Tuesday.

This has only been happening **since** the new software was installed.

The measures will hopefully be in place **from** Tuesday.

The office is open **from** 9:00 until 12:00 noon at the weekend.

C. It is likely to take longer than six weeks.

from six weeks   ~~within six weeks~~   ~~in six weeks~~   after six weeks
~~for six weeks~~   ~~up to six weeks~~   ~~at six weeks~~

It is likely to last six weeks.

~~from six weeks~~   within six weeks   ~~in six weeks~~   ~~after six weeks~~
for six weeks   up to six weeks   ~~at six weeks~~

It will start around six weeks' time.

from six weeks   ~~within six weeks~~   in six weeks   ~~after six weeks~~
~~for six weeks~~   ~~up to six weeks~~   at six weeks

Answers to Chapter 16 (16.8)

A. The 19th section of the report lists the occasions when this can occur. CORRECT

Brooks, C. 2014. *Introductory Econometrics for Finance*. 3rd ed. Cambridge: Cambridge University Press. CORRECT

The ~~forth~~ (**fourth**) reason is related to location, and the fifth reason is external investment.

~~19 out of 60~~ (**Nineteen out of sixty**) of the studies reviewed rejected the hypothesis put forward by Klinger (2002).

The company came ~~seven~~ (**seventh**) in a list of the top ten companies in revenue.

Almost three-quarters of the respondents 'strongly agreed' with this statement. CORRECT

B. These are all written as a **percentage**.

Sixty-seven **percent** were absent on the final day.

At least 60**%** are in favour.

The **percentage** of people who then report this has decreased though.

Answers to Chapter 17 (17.4)

A. Table 4 below shows the relationships among the four variables. CORRECT

This is shown in Table 7 below. CORRECT

According to the table below, the only support the scheme received was from Morgan (2006). CORRECT

B. The following **table (6.3)** presents the findings of our study.

This **is demonstrated** in **Figures 3.1–3.4** above.

The previous model (4.1) **presented** the four algorithms.

The diagram below (Figure 7) outlines these provisions.

Answers to Chapter 18 (18.3)

A. Every project must go **through** different **phases** with different teams involved. This next section **identifies** the phases in which the **management** team feature to **form** an overall picture of their role and influence. **Previously** we looked at the design teams and how they **aligned** their ideas with the production team. The aim is to create a product that the **customer** identifies with. This is **where** feedback is also important, so the teams can **learn** about what the customer desires.

Answers to Chapter 19 (19.6)

A. The dissertation is divided into five chapters. In this chapter I introduced the rationale and the aims of this study from which the research questions were drawn.

The final objective is to understand learners' perceptions of the text, which ties in with objective three.

The authors would like to thank Mr Michael Morgan for his feedback on the model. We would also like to thank Orion Solutions for lending us the equipment to carry out the experiments. The first experiment used their original RH200 system; the second experiment required the upgrade.

The UK and China are two other countries that have well-established trading relationships (Huang 2010, pp. 23–45).

The leverage is positively related to these tax shields in the real estate industry, although the outcome is not statistically significant.

The participants are studying subjects at the Arts School—primarily Graphics and Illustration—in the south of the district.

B. When we were informed that there would only be four people in the **focus group**, we were not expecting the group to be that informative. According to Chen (1998), from his book *Research Methods in Action*, such a small group was unlikely to generate the **group dynamics** necessary for an outstanding session; **however**, the focus group actually turned out to be very informative, and all the questions we prepared for the **discussion** were fully answered with interesting insights from the **participants**.

Answers to Chapter 20 (20.6)

A. Cho (2006: 61) rejects Tan's (1998) view of enterprise zones.

Smith et al. (2014) question the quality of student feedback in UK universities.

B. Johnson et al. (2007) reviewed 19 definitions of mixed-methods and concluded that *'mixed-methods research . . . combines elements of qualitative and quantitative research approaches . . . and helps to develop a more complete understanding of the topic (p. 123).'*

INDEX

By term

B = Background section of a chapter (e.g., 1B = Background section of Chapter 1)
1.1 = Chapter 1, section 1
A = Appendix